Oracle BAM 11gR1 Handbook

Your essential BAM sidekick for monitoring, alerting, and application best practices with Oracle Business Activity Monitoring

Pete Wang

BIRMINGHAM - MUMBAI

Oracle BAM 11gR1 Handbook

First published: April 2012

Production Reference: 1280312

Published by Packt Publishing Ltd.
Livery Place
35 Livery Street
Birmingham B3 2PB, UK.

ISBN 978-1-84968-544-3

www.packtpub.com

Cover Image by Sandeep Babu (sandyjb@gmail.com)

Credits

Author
Pete Wang

Reviewers
Vaibhav Shankar Ambavale

Martijn van der Kamp

Arun Pareek

Jan-Willem Pas

Acquisition Editor
Stephanie Moss

Lead Technical Editor
Shreerang Deshpande

Technical Editor
Lubna Shaikh

Project Coordinator
Joel Goveya

Proofreader
Aaron Nash

Indexer
Hemangini Bari

Graphics
Manu Joseph

Valentina D'souza

Production Coordinator
Aparna Bhagat

Prachali Bhiwandkar

Cover Work
Aparna Bhagat

Foreword

As businesses are increasing their use of **Service Oriented Architecture (SOA)** to build their core business systems, the need for real-time visibility into their business processes is becoming critical. At the same time, IT budgets are shrinking, and businesses are under constant pressure to cut costs and optimize their investments. **Oracle Business Activity Monitoring (Oracle BAM)** provides a comprehensive solution for building real-time dashboards and alerts for monitoring **Service Level Agreements (SLAs)** and other **Key Performance Indicators (KPIs)**.

Like Oracle SOA Suite and Oracle BPM Suite, Oracle BAM 11g leverages the best-of-breed WebLogic Server platform to achieve a high quality of service. As a completely new release, Oracle BAM 11g offers many new features and enhancements in the areas of usability, performance, scalability, and interoperability.

The book is a comprehensive handbook that focuses on providing guidance and best practices for building BAM applications including designing, developing, and troubleshooting. The key topics covered in the book are:

- Oracle BAM 11g concepts and architecture
- Developing and load testing BAM applications
- Configuring an LDAP server and SSL for BAM
- Migrating BAM applications from one environment to another
- Troubleshooting and tuning BAM applications
- Configuring BAM High Availability

This book provides an in-depth coverage of Oracle BAM 11g, as well as troubleshooting methodologies that can be used for advanced problem resolution. The BAM samples for this book help solidify the readers' understanding of the concepts through hands-on experience.

All the instructions, guidelines, tips, best practices, and cases studies are based on real-world problems and solutions. By following these best practices, SOA developers can significantly increase their productivity, avoid common pitfalls, and create more agile, scalable, and reusable BAM applications.

As the global technical lead for BAM and a member of the A-Team, Pete's real-world experience with SOA and BAM-based solutions helps keep the book grounded in practical solutions to real-world challenges that companies face.

Focusing on accurate, pragmatic instructions, and best practices, this book should be a perfect guide for SOA architects and developers, in developing and administrating BAM applications.

Robert Patrick

Vice President, Oracle Fusion Middleware Architects Team: The A-Team

About the Author

Pete Wang is a member of the Oracle Fusion Middleware Architects team: the A-Team that focuses on managing all aspects of the SOA/AIA engagements, including proof of concepts, support escalations, sales engagement, user conferences, seminars, workshops, and so on. With a well-established credibility and influence in the area of SOA/BAM, Pete is a trusted advisor, and plays a key technical role in guiding customers, consultants, support analysts, and engineers in resolving critical customer and product issues. Prior to the A-Team role, Pete took on various roles in Customer Support and Sales Consulting at both Oracle and BEA Systems.

Pete has over 12 years of experience in the design and the development of SOA/BAM/JavaEE applications, and he specializes in designing and troubleshooting large-scale and mission-critical systems built with various middleware technologies. As the **Global Technical Lead (GTL)** for BAM in Support, Pete has been actively engaged in delivering BAM solutions, publishing articles, support escalations, and advanced resolutions, to ensure the success of customers.

Pete is currently living in Melbourne, Australia, but will move to Boston, MA, USA, with his family soon. Pete holds a Master's Degree in Information Science from the University of New South Wales, Australia, and he likes to play tennis and soccer in his spare time.

Acknowledgement

First of all, I would like to take this opportunity to express my sincere gratitude to all the members of the BAM Development team and the Oracle management team, especially to Robert Patrick, Jeff McDaniel, Payal Srivastava, Stephen Sherman, Hani Isac, and Odin Grupe for their support, encouragement, and guidance throughout the development of this book.

I would also like to express my deep gratitude to all the contributors and the reviewers, who truly play a key part in improving the contents and making this book complete. Their hard work, great ideas, and precious comments really make a difference. Special thanks to Michael Zhao who has spent a lot of his spare time in building and testing the samples, thus ensuring the high quality of the code and instructions. Without their contributions, this book wouldn't have been as good as it is now.

I would like to say a big thank you to the team at Packt Publishing, who are always willing to help with their professionalism, enthusiasm, and dedication. Special thanks go to Stephanie Moss, who provided a lot of invaluable feedback and comments in the early stage of writing, which really made my job easier as an author.

Finally, I would like to dedicate this book to my lovely wife, Daisy, who has been supporting and encouraging me throughout the course of the book's development. Without her continued support, patience, and care, I would not have pursued and completed this work in such a short amount of time.

About the Reviewers

Vaibhav Shankar Ambavale is a solution architect, and has extensive experience in Middleware technologies. He is passionate about designing and developing applications. He is an Oracle certified Expert on Oracle SOA suite 11g. He has expertise in Oracle Fusion middleware – SOA, BPM, BAM, mediator, B2B, AIA, and WebLogic. He has extensive experience in the B2B domain, where he worked on various B2B products and protocols.

Besides work, he enjoys traveling, trekking, and photography. Vaibhav holds a Bachelor's degree in engineering from V.J.T.I., Mumbai, India.

Martijn van der Kamp is an enthusiastic Oracle specialist from the Netherlands. His focus is on the Fusion Middleware stack. When he started working for Capgemini, he got in touch with Oracle BPM. Quickly, his interest transformed to passion.

Martijn has worked on several (international) projects in the Oracle BPM domain, where he gained expertise and knowledge of implementing BAM.

I would like to thank Léon Smiers for getting me acquainted with, and coaching me on, Oracle BPM and BAM.

Arun Pareek is a SOA practitioner, working on SOA-based implementation projects in the capacity of a consultant and architect for over five years now. He is also an IASA certified software architect, and is currently co-authoring a book on Oracle SOA Suite Administration for Packt Publishing. He has been actively working on the SOA Suite of products of both BEA and Oracle, including technologies such as Service Bus, AIA, BPEL, BAM, BPA, and BPMN. He has a knack for designing systems that are scalable, performant, and fault-tolerant, and is an enthusiast for automated continuous integration techniques. He is also an active blogger on these technologies, and runs a popular blog at `http://beatechnologies.wordpress.com`.

I would like to appreciate the encouragement I received from my parents for helping me achieve many things in my life. A special note of thanks goes to my wonderful wife Karuna for her constant support, cooperation, and patience, without which, it wouldn't have been possible for me to manage my work and life together.

Jan-Willem Pas is a Database and Integration specialist working at Capgemini, Netherlands.

After completing his Bachelor's degrees in Technical IT and Commercial Engineering and Management, Mr. Pas started working as a software developer/designer for numerous customers, and in numerous environments, using Oracle Database technology and other classic Oracle products, such as Reports, Forms, and Workflow.

Gradually, he began to focus more on SOA/Integration projects, mainly using the Oracle technology. During his last major project, Mr. Pas has participated in a BPM Work Order management implementation for a big customer in the Dutch energy sector, using the latest Oracle products, such as BPM, OSB, BI Publisher, and Oracle BAM.

His role has grown into a more functional and leading one, and he is now responsible for leading the development team that continues the maintenance and the development of this Work Order management system.

www.PacktPub.com

Support files, eBooks, discount offers and more

You might want to visit www.PacktPub.com for support files and downloads related to your book.

Did you know that Packt offers eBook versions of every book published, with PDF and ePub files available? You can upgrade to the eBook version at www.PacktPub.com and as a print book customer, you are entitled to a discount on the eBook copy. Get in touch with us at service@packtpub.com for more details.

At www.PacktPub.com, you can also read a collection of free technical articles, sign up for a range of free newsletters and receive exclusive discounts and offers on Packt books and eBooks.

http://PacktLib.PacktPub.com

Do you need instant solutions to your IT questions? PacktLib is Packt's online digital book library. Here, you can access, read and search across Packt's entire library of books.

Why Subscribe?

- Fully searchable across every book published by Packt
- Copy and paste, print and bookmark content
- On demand and accessible via web browser

Free Access for Packt account holders

If you have an account with Packt at www.PacktPub.com, you can use this to access PacktLib today and view nine entirely free books. Simply use your login credentials for immediate access.

Instant Updates on New Packt Books

Get notified! Find out when new books are published by following @PacktEnterprise on Twitter, or the *Packt Enterprise* Facebook page.

Table of Contents

Preface

An integral component of Oracle SOA and BPM Suite, Oracle BAM Business Activity Monitoring (BAM) ultimately empowers business executives to react quickly to the changing business situations. BAM enables business service and process monitoring through real-time data streaming and operational reports, and this book helps you to take advantage of this vital tool with best practice guidance for building a BAM project.

Oracle BAM 11gR1 Handbook is an essential companion for advancing your BAM knowledge, with troubleshooting and performance tuning tips to guide you in building BAM applications.

The book uses step-by-step instructions alongside a real world demo project to steer you through the pitfalls of report and application development. Packed with best practices, you'll learn about BAM migration, HA configuration, and much more.

This book comprises a myriad of best practices for building real-time operational dashboards, reports, and alerts.

The book dives straight into the architecture of Oracle BAM 11g, before moving swiftly onto concepts like managing BAM server securities, populating Data Objects, and performing load testing. Later on you'll also learn about BAM migration and building an ADF-based report, plus much more that you won't want to miss.

For focusing in on best practices for this integral tool within Oracle SOA and BPM Suite, *Oracle BAM 11gR1 Handbook* is the perfect guide for the job.

What this book covers

Chapter 1, BAM 11gR1 Architecture, introduces the Oracle BAM key concepts, and its high-level architecture.

Chapter 2, Designing your First Data Objects and Reports, covers the basics for designing your Data Objects and reports.

Chapter 3, *Populating Data Objects with Real-time Data*, explores various technologies, such as **Enterprise Message Sources** (**EMS**), the Oracle BAM Adapter, BPEL Sensors, and Oracle BAM Web services, which can be used to move the business data to BAM.

Chapter 4, *Designing BAM Reports*, covers the techniques/procedures for designing BAM reports with multiple views to meet your business needs.

Chapter 5, *Testing BAM Applications*, discusses the testing methodology in general, and the BAM-specific methodology for conducting end-to-end testing under normal and load condition.

Chapter 6, *Managing BAM Securities*, discusses the key BAM security concepts, which include authentication, authorization, and SSL.

Chapter 7, *Migrating BAM to a Different Environment*, discusses the best practices for migrating BAM to a different environment.

Chapter 8, *Configuring High Availability for BAM*, discusses the Oracle BAM high availability solution/best practices in the Application Server tier.

Chapter 9, *Troubleshooting your BAM Applications*, explores the troubleshooting techniques, methodologies, and case studies.

Chapter 10, *Building your Reports Using ADF*, discusses how to build reports using the Oracle **Application Development Framework** (**ADF**).

What you need for this book

Hardware requirements:

- At least 2G memory, 4G is recommended.

Software requirements:

- Oracle SOA Suite 11.1.1.4 or later releases.
- Oracle JDeveloper 11.1.1.4 or later releases. Ensure that the JDeveloper release matches the SOA Suite.
- Microsoft Internet Explorer (IE) browser (7.0 or later release) on your host OS.

Who this book is for

If you are a developer/report developer or SOA Architect who wants to learn valuable Oracle BAM best practices for monitoring your operations in real time, then Oracle BAM 11gR1 Handbook is for you. Administrators will also find the book useful.

You should already be comfortable with SOA architecture and SQL practices.

Conventions

In this book, you will find a number of styles of text that distinguish between different kinds of information. Here are some examples of these styles, and an explanation of their meaning.

Code words in text are shown as follows: " Let us look at a `ChangeList` example, which is produced by a ViewSet of the `Employees` Data Object."

A block of code is set as follows:

```
<ADCServerName>localhost</ADCServerName>
<ADCServerPort>9001</ADCServerPort>
<ICommand_Default_User_Name>user</ICommand_Default_User_Name>
<ICommand_Default_Password>passwd</ICommand_Default_Password>
```

When we wish to draw your attention to a particular part of a code block, the relevant lines or items are set in bold:

```
<S:Envelope xmlns:S="http://schemas.xmlsoap.org/soap/envelope/">
  <S:Header>
    <work:WorkContext
      xmlns:work="http://oracle.com/weblogic/soap/workarea/">
      rO0ABXdOABd3ZWJsb2dpYy5hcHAub3JhY2xLWWJhbQAAANYAAAA
        jd2VibG9naWMud29ya2FyZWEuU3RyaW5nV29ya0NvbnRleHQABjExLjEuMQAA
    </work:WorkContext>
  </S:Header>
  <S:Body>
    <ns2:InsertResponse xmlns:ns2="http://xmlns.oracle.com/bam"/>
  </S:Body>
</S:Envelope>
```

Any command-line input or output is written as follows:

```
SOA_HOME/bam/bin/icommand.bat -CMD IMPORT -FILE <file name>
```

New terms and **important words** are shown in bold. Words that you see on the screen, in menus or dialog boxes for example, appear in the text like this: " Among them, **Active Data Cache**, **Report Cache**, and **Report Server** are the major components that are responsible for static and dynamic report rendering ".

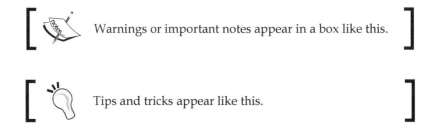

Warnings or important notes appear in a box like this.

Tips and tricks appear like this.

Reader feedback

Feedback from our readers is always welcome. Let us know what you think about this book—what you liked or may have disliked. Reader feedback is important for us to develop titles that you really get the most out of.

To send us general feedback, simply send an e-mail to feedback@packtpub.com, and mention the book title through the subject of your message.

If there is a topic that you have expertise in and you are interested in either writing or contributing to a book, see our author guide on www.packtpub.com/authors.

Customer support

Now that you are the proud owner of a Packt book, we have a number of things to help you to get the most from your purchase.

Downloading the example code

You can download the example code files for all Packt books you have purchased from your account at http://www.packtpub.com. If you purchased this book elsewhere, you can visit http://www.packtpub.com/support and register to have the files e-mailed directly to you.

Errata

Although we have taken every care to ensure the accuracy of our content, mistakes do happen. If you find a mistake in one of our books—maybe a mistake in the text or the code—we would be grateful if you would report this to us. By doing so, you can save other readers from frustration and help us improve subsequent versions of this book. If you find any errata, please report them by visiting http://www.packtpub.com/support, selecting your book, clicking on the **errata submission form** link, and entering the details of your errata. Once your errata are verified, your submission will be accepted and the errata will be uploaded to our website, or added to any list of existing errata, under the Errata section of that title.

Piracy

Piracy of copyright material on the Internet is an ongoing problem across all media. At Packt, we take the protection of our copyright and licenses very seriously. If you come across any illegal copies of our works, in any form, on the Internet, please provide us with the location address or website name immediately so that we can pursue a remedy.

Please contact us at copyright@packtpub.com with a link to the suspected pirated material.

We appreciate your help in protecting our authors, and our ability to bring you valuable content.

Questions

You can contact us at questions@packtpub.com if you are having a problem with any aspect of the book, and we will do our best to address it.

1
BAM 11gR1 Architecture

Oracle **Business Activity Monitoring (BAM)** 11g R1 architecture leverages the push-based mechanism to deliver the high volume of data changes to the frontend web browser in real time, which is the key differentiator from other conventional reporting solutions that use the pulling approach for report rendering.

To help you understand the push-based mechanism and BAM Architecture, this chapter first introduces BAM key concepts, which are the prerequisites to learning BAM. We will then discuss an overview of the architecture, and its key server side components. Finally, you will see an explanation of the message flows in typical report opening and data change scenarios, so that you can understand what happens behind the scenes.

Oracle BAM key concepts

In this section, we will give you a brief review of the key concepts, which will help you to gain a better understanding of BAM Architecture, and more advanced topics.

Data Object

A **Data Object** is an internal data structure that represents the business data in the BAM server. Like the concept of the database tables, a Data Object has a flat structure, which includes fields with primitive data types, such as `string`, `integer`, `float`, `date time`, and so on. It can also include calculated fields and lookup fields, which reference to other Data Objects using foreign keys. The Data Object field cannot be defined using complex data types, such as arrays, objects, and so on.

The following screenshot depicts the `Employees` Data Object layout, which is defined using simple primitive data types, such as `string`, `integer`, and `timestamp`:

Field name	Field ID	Field type	Max length	Scale	Nullable	Public	Lookup	Calculated	Tip Text
Salesperson	_Salesperson	string	100	-	Yes	Yes	-	-	-
Sales Area	_Sales_Area	string	100	-	Yes	Yes	-	-	-
Sales Number	_Sales_Number	integer	-	-	Yes	Yes	-	-	-
Timestamp	_Timestamp	timestamp	-	-	No	Yes	-	-	-

Data Objects are managed in the in-memory data cache to meet the needs of high volume data processing, and get persistent in the BAM database schema automatically. In the current release, Oracle BAM supports the following RDBMS as its persistence store: Oracle Database, IBM DB2, and Microsoft SQL server.

More Data Object details will be covered in *Chapter 2*, *Designing your First Data Objects and Reports*.

ViewSet

A **ViewSet** is an object that represents a query to a given Data Object. A `ViewSet` provides an abstraction layer that decouples the View design and underlying data model, which allows multiple reports to share the same Data Object.

In BAM, a `ViewSet` is defined using an XML schema, which can contain the following elements:

- `ViewSetID`: A unique identifier for one particular `ViewSet`
- `ViewsetSchema`: A schema definition root element which can contain:
    - `DatasetField`: A field defined in Data Object
    - `CalculatedField`: A field defined in the `ViewSet`, but not in Data Object
    - `AggregateField`: An aggregate, such as sum, average, and so on

To understand this concept, let's take a look at an example that represents the query to the `Employee` Data Object that you saw before.

```
<View>
  <ViewSetID>b5bdcb24408df9fb11b855741317ae6e9b8-75a5</ViewSetID>
  <ViewsetSchema dataset="_Employees" id="0" viewsetID="">
    <DatasetField dataType="STRING" datasetField="_Sales_Area"
                  fieldID="" fieldRefID="0"/>
    <AggregateField fieldID="SUM(_Sales_Number)" fieldRefID="1"
                    operandfieldRefID="2" operation="SUM"/>
    <DatasetField dataType="FLOAT" datasetField="_Sales_Number" fieldRefID="2"/>
  </ViewsetSchema>
</View>
```

In this `ViewSet` definition, the dataset attribute specifies the database table (`_Employees`) that is used to persist the Data Object (`Employee`). The `DatasetField` and `AggregateField` elements specify the `_Sales_Area` data field and the aggregate `SUM(_Sales_Number)` that can be used to construct the query to the `_Employees` dataset.

`ViewSets` can also be sorted, filtered, and applied row-level securities. More topics related to `ViewSet` will be covered in the next chapter.

View

A **View** is a rendered result set, which is generated by opening one or a collection of `ViewSets`. The following is a sample of the 3D bar chart View that shows the number of orders, grouped by its status:

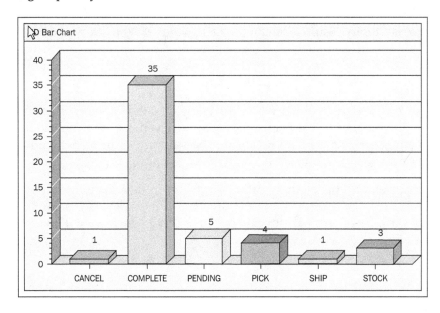

In the current BAM release, a View can only be rendered in the IE browser. The View type specific XSL transformation, which is used to convert report data to DHTML with JavaScript, utilizes proprietary IE features that are not available in other web browsers, such as Firefox, Chrome, and so on.

The list of View types supported in BAM 11g R1 include the following:

- Charts: Area chart, bar chart, combo chart, funnel chart, line chart, pie chart, SPC chart, and stacked bar chart
- Lists: Streaming list, updating list, updating ordered list, and collapsed list
- Action Form
- Columnar
- Dashboard
- Row group, column group
- KPIs: Arrow, market arrow, dial gauge, range gauge
- Tab group
- Excel spreadsheet

You will learn more about these View types in *Chapter 4*, .

Snapshot

A **Snapshot** is a query result set created by a ViewSet. When a report is first rendered, a ViewSet is opened to generate the initial result, which is called a Snapshot. The XML representation of the Snapshot is then transformed to DHTML using View-specific XSL, and sent to the client along with JavaScript.

Snapshots are cached in the BAM Server. So, every time the same report is opened in another browser session, the Snapshot will be retrieved, and sent back to the client without generating from scratch, which helps improve the report rendering performance.

Snapshots can be used to generate static Views. To produce dynamic Views, or in other words, to render a report that can reflect the data changes in real time, you will need a push-based mechanism called Active Data, which we will look at next.

Active Data

Active Data is the continuous stream of changes that the ViewSet can produce. Once a report is first rendered with a Snapshot, any subsequent changes to the Snapshot of the ViewSet will be captured at the server side, and pushed back to the client. This is what we call a **push-based mechanism**.

A push-based mechanism is an efficient way of delivering real-time notifications to the client. Unlike the polling approach, in which clients need to consistently send requests to the server, Active Data allows the server to send the changed data in an incremental way, instead of transferring all the report data to the client, and thus can provide significant advantages, such as the following:

- Leveraging client and server resources more efficiently
- Significantly reducing the network traffic
- Fast rendering report with Active Data

You will learn more about Active Data and push-based mechanisms in the *Understanding message flow* section, later in this chapter.

ChangeList

A **ChangeList** is an Active Data Payload that includes the changes produced by a specific ViewSet.

The ChangeList is in XML format, which normally includes the following:

- index: A sequence number of a ChangeList. When a report is first rendered, a ViewSet will be opened with a Snapshot. Any further Data Object changes may trigger a ChangeList generated with incremental index numbers starting from one. The index will increment by one as any new changes come.

- viewsetID: A unique identifier for a particular ViewSet, the index, and viewsetID together identify the ChangeList.

- Group: A container to hold ChangeList records.

- Record: An XML element representing a row in the updated query result of a ViewSet. A Record contains a transaction type (insert, update, upsert, and delete), Data Object field references, and contents.

Let us look at a `ChangeList` example, which is produced by a `ViewSet` of the `Employees` Data Object.

```
<ChangeList index="1" viewsetID="b5bdcb24408df9fb11b855741317ae6e9b8-7432">
  <Group count="3" id="0" level="0" pos="0" xnType="update">">
    <Record id="1" pos="0" xnType="update">
      <Field fieldID="0" fieldRefID="0">Northeast
        <FormattedValue>Northeast</FormattedValue>
      </Field>
      <Field fieldID="1" fieldRefID="1">568
        <FormattedValue>568</FormattedValue>
      </Field>
      <Field fieldID="2" fieldRefID="2">Greg Masters
        <FormattedValue>Greg Masters</FormattedValue>
      </Field>
      <Field fieldID="3" fieldRefID="3">2011-08-10T22:23:37.1420000+10:00
        <FormattedValue>8/10/2011 10:23:37 PM</FormattedValue>
      </Field>
    </Record>
  </Group>
</ChangeList>
```

The key points that you can see from the example are:

- The `ChangeList` sequence number is identified by the `index` attribute value. `1` means this is the first `ChangeList` for the `ViewSet`.

- The `Field` definition and `FormattedValue` provide the detailed information for the `ChangeList` contents.

- The `xnType` attribute defined in the `Record` element specifies the transaction type (update) for the `Record` of the `ChangeList`. The other possible transaction type values are `insert`, `upsert`, and `delete`.

 Throughout the rest of the book, we will use the terms Active Data and ChangeList interchangeably.

BAM 11gR1 architecture

In this section, we will introduce a BAM11gR1 high level architecture, and the overview of its components.

Architecture overview

BAM server is a Java EE application deployed to Weblogic Server. As shown in the following diagram, BAM server contains the following components:

- **Active Data Cache**
- **Messaging Framework**
- **Enterprise Messaging Sources (EMS)**
- **Report Cache**
- **Report Server**
- **Event Engine**
- **BAM Web Applications**
- **BAM Web Services**

Among them, **Active Data Cache**, **Report Cache**, and **Report Server** are the major components that are responsible for static and dynamic report rendering.

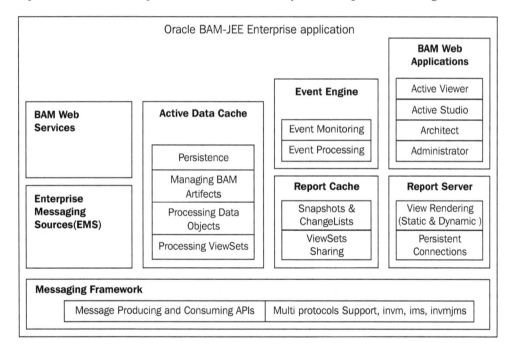

BAM server components

In this section, you will see an overview of BAM server components, what these server components are, and what services they provide.

Active Data Cache

Oracle BAM **Active Data Cache** (**ADC**) is the key BAM server component and is a high-performance, persistent, and memory-based storage system, designed to support data model management and Active Data processing.

Active Data Cache is the component that receives continuous data streams from various data sources, such as BPEL processes, SOA composites, JMS queues or topics, databases, enterprise information systems, legacy applications, and so on. It also provides the following services, which are explained as follows:

- Persistence
- Maintaining BAM artifacts
- Managing data models
- Processing Active Data

Persistence

Continuous data streams received by BAM are converted to the corresponding data models, which are persistent in the backend repository. BAM 11gR1 supports Oracle, DB2, and Microsoft SQL server as the repository. The repository is created using **Repository Creation Utility** (**RCU**). The usage of RCU is out of the scope of this book, and you can find more information about RCU in the *Oracle Fusion Middleware Repository Creation Utility User's Guide 11g Release 1 (11.1.1)*. Note that documentation link varies on different releases. On 11.1.1.6 release, this document can be accessed at the following URL:

`http://docs.oracle.com/cd/E23943_01/doc.1111/e14259/toc.htm`.

Maintaining BAM artifacts

BAM artifacts are the metadata stored in the repository. Examples of BAM artifacts are Data Objects, reports, users, and roles.

Oracle BAM schema contains a list of tables starting with `SysIter`, which represent system tables storing the metadata. For example, the `SysIterReport` table stores `Report` metadata, such as report definition, the created date, last modified date, and so on.

BAM artifacts are internal concepts and definitions, and it is not recommended to modify these artifacts by directly manipulating system tables. The preferred way of maintaining BAM artifacts is through the appropriate GUI tools provided by BAM.

Managing data models

BAM ADC provides methods for creating, modifying, and deleting BAM Data Objects. It also provides APIs to insert, update, upsert, and delete data into Data Objects.

This is a very important feature provided by ADC, and you will learn how to manage data models in the next chapter.

> APIs used to manage data models are exposed by Session EJB, called `BamServerBean`. These APIs are used internally by BAM web applications, such as Architect, other BAM server components, and BAM sensors and adapters. When attempting to feed live data into BAM, data is passed through existing channels, such as BAM adapter, BAM web service interface, ODI, or Enterprise Message Sources, which in turn call `BamServerBean` APIs.

Processing Active Data

Handling Active Data is the key capability of BAM ADC. As you saw earlier, Active Data represents the changes to the Snapshot of the ViewSet.

Processing Active Data is complex, and you will learn more about it in the following chapters.

Messaging framework

Messaging framework is a common messaging layer that provides producing and consuming message services, which are used by other BAM server components.

As shown in the architecture diagram, the Messaging Framework provides a messaging backbone that allows different server components to communicate with each other in an asynchronous way. For example, when Active Data are pushed from ADC to other components, it will be sent to an internal queue through the Messaging Framework.

While understanding this concept will help you troubleshoot messaging related issues, you will not directly use Messaging Framework APIs when building your BAM applications. You will learn more about the Messaging Framework in *Chapter 3, Populating Data Objects with Real-time Data*.

Enterprise Message Sources

Enterprise Message Sources (**EMS**) provides direct **Java Message Service** (**JMS**) connectivity to Oracle BAM server, by mapping messages directly to Oracle BAM Data Objects. Oracle BAM server can read data directly from any JMS-based message queue or topic through the Messaging Framework.

EMS allows mapping from an XML message directly to a Data Object on Oracle BAM server, however, you may use XSL transformations before the data is inserted, updated, upserted, or deleted into the Data Object. Each EMS consumes messages from a specific JMS topic or a queue, and the information is delivered into a Data Object in Oracle BAM ADC.

The Oracle BAM Architect web application is used to configure EMS definitions. You will learn more about EMS in *Chapter 3*.

Report Cache

Oracle BAM **Report Cache** off-loads the burden of maintaining the `ViewSet` Snapshot in memory from Oracle BAM Active Data Cache. Report Cache opens `ViewSets`, and caches the Snapshot and the ChangeList before sending it to the Report Server. This allows for random access into the Snapshot, and recovery from losing Internet connectivity.

Report Cache also allows for the Oracle BAM Report Server to be stateless.

Event Engine

The **Event Engine** monitors complex data conditions, and implements user-defined rules. The Event Engine continuously monitors the information in the ADC for certain conditions, and executes the related actions defined in associated rules. It takes a variety of actions in response to those changes, including notifying the appropriate user with an alert and/or report(s).

Report Server

Oracle BAM Report Server renders static and active reports. It also manages persistent connections between the web browser clients and BAM server.

Oracle BAM Report Server applies the report definitions to the data sets retrieved from the Oracle BAM Report Cache for presentation in a browser. It manages information paging for viewing and printing reports.

BAM web applications

Oracle BAM web applications are a set of web-based interfaces for building and managing data models, creating Views and reports, viewing reports, and performing administrative tasks. The BAM web applications include the following:

- **Start page**: A GUI tool that provides a login screen and single access point to Oracle web applications

- **Active viewer**: A GUI tool for browsing and viewing reports

- **Active studio**: A GUI tool for designing reports and alerts

- **Architect**: A GUI tool for managing Data Objects, enterprise messaging sources, external data sources, and alerts

- **Administrator**: A GUI tool for viewing users and roles

 From the perspective of the user's experience, BAM 11g web applications remain the same as those of BAM 10g, except for the Administrator web application, in which you can only view BAM users and roles in BAM 11gR1. The reason is that BAM 11gR1 dedicates the user management to the WebLogic server console, and the role management to Oracle enterprise manager fusion middleware control. Thus, the Administrator web application only provides a read-only view of the existing users and roles. You will learn more about BAM Securities in *Chapter 6, Managing BAM Securities*.

Understanding message flow

In this section, we will dive into the BAM server components to help you to understand what happens behind the scenes in the following scenarios:

- Opening a report for the first time
- Processing Active Data

Opening a report for the first time

This is the scenario when a user attempts to open a report for the first time.

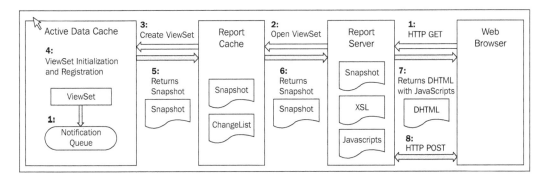

This diagram depicts the message flow, which can be interpreted as follows:

1. The client sends an **HTTP** request containing report definition ID and a list of parameters to the **Report Server**. An example request is something like:

```
http://<bam_server_hostname>:<port>/OracleBAM/reportserver/
default.jsp?Event=viewReport&ReportDef=58&Buttons=False&ReportP
arameters=()
```

   In this URL, `<bam_server_hostname>` is the BAM server hostname, `ReportDef` is a parameter that specifies the report `ID`, and `ReportParameters` is an HTTP request parameter that specifies report parameters.

2. The **Report Server** processes the request, then invokes the **Report Cache** method to open a **ViewSet**.

3. Since this is the first time a **ViewSet** is opened, the **Report Cache** invokes **Active Data Cache** APIs to create a **ViewSet**.

4. The **Active Data Cache** instantiates the ViewSet, and registers it as a listener to the associated Data Object **Notification Queue**.

5. The **Active Data Cache** builds and executes SQL queries, and returns the initial result set (**Snapshot**) to the **Report Cache**.

6. The **Report Cache** saves the opened **Viewset** and associated Snapshot in the cache, and then passes the **ViewSet** and **Snapshot** to the **Report Server**.

7. The **Report Server** transforms the **Snapshot** to DHTML, using View specific **XSL**, and sends it to the client along with **JavaScript** for rendering.

8. After the initial View is rendered successfully in the web browser, the View generates a `getChangeList()` request, and sends it through **HTTP POST** to **Report Server ActiveDataServlet**.

> **Why does the client send a separate HTTP request to BAM Report Server after a View is rendered for the first time?**
>
> BAM report leverages a push-based mechanism to receive Active Data in real time. After a report is first rendered in a web browser, it has to find out a way to register the View to the Report Server, which maintains persistent connections between the client and BAM Server. Sending the `getChangeList()` request to `ActiveDataServlet` creates the persistent connection through which the Active Data changes are pushed.

Processing Active Data

Up to now, we have mentioned many times that BAM server uses the push-based mechanism to process Active Data. In this section, we will use a diagram to illustrate how Active Data are processed by BAM server components:

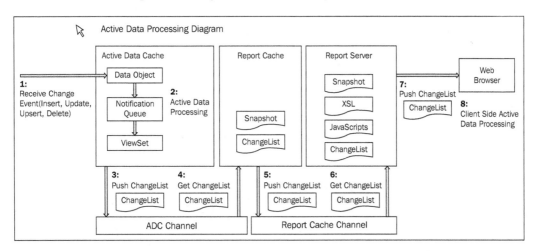

As shown in this diagram, Active Data processing message flows are as follows:

1. The **Active Data Cache** receives a data change Event (**Insert**, **Update**, **Upsert**, and **Delete**) that happens to one of its managed **Data Objects**.

2. The **Active Data Cache** persists the change to the repository, and raises an Event to notify the changes to **ViewSet**, which is listening on particular Events in the notification queue.

3. The **Active Data Cache** calculates how the change is affecting the specific continuous query that it is running for the user, and in the end, it will generate a **ChangeList**, and push it through the **Messaging Framework** for asynchronous delivery.

4. The **Report Cache** gets notified when the **ChangeList** arrives, consumes the XML payload through the **Messaging Framework**, and saves it into its internal cache.

5. The **Report Cache** pushes the **ChangeList** to the **Report Cache Channel**, which is an internal or JMS topic.

6. The **Report Server** receives the **ChangeList** from the **Report Cache Channel**.

7. The **Report Server** sends the **ChangeList** to the client through the persistent connection established by `ActiveDataServlet` that you saw before.

8. Client side JavaScript receives the `ChangeList`, and then updates the Views opened in the browser to reflect the changes in real time.

Summary

In this chapter, we covered BAM key concepts, the architecture overview, BAM server components, and most importantly, the message flows that happen, given two typical scenarios in BAM.

In the next chapter, we will dive into Active Data Cache, discuss more Data Object related concepts, and provide instructions and best practices for building, extending, and managing Data Objects.

2
Designing Your First Data Objects and Reports

In the first chapter, we introduced Oracle BAM key concepts and its architecture. You may have found these topics to be quite abstract and complex, so to help solidify your understanding of these important concepts, and gain some experience with the development of BAM applications, we will guide you through the steps to build your first Data Object and report, and start sharing tips and tricks for building BAM applications.

In this chapter, you will first learn how to design your first Data Object, including Data Object design considerations, creating Data Objects, adding lookup fields, and creating external Data Objects. Then, you will learn how to create a single View report, based on the Data Objects you created.

In order to demonstrate the best practices for building BAM applications, we have developed samples, which can be found in the book's samples folder. As each chapter may use its own sample code and data, we recommend that you follow the instructions carefully in the README.txt file associated with every sample.

The prerequisites for running BAM samples are as follows:

- Download and install Oracle SOA Suite (11.1.1.4 or later release).
- Download and install Oracle JDeveloper (11.1.1.4 or later release). Ensure that the JDeveloper release matches the SOA Suite.
- Ensure that you have installed Microsoft **Internet Explorer** (**IE**) browser (7.0 or later release) on your host OS.

Designing your first Data Objects

As you saw in the *BAM key concepts* section, in the previous chapter, BAM Data Objects represent data models, which are used to create reports in Oracle BAM Active Studio. Each Data Object has a specific layout that can be a combination of data fields, lookup fields, and calculated fields.

In this section, you will learn how to design your first Data Objects. First, let's get started with the BAM Architect web application.

Getting started with the BAM Architect web application

The **BAM Architect Web application** is a GUI tool for managing Data Objects, enterprise messaging sources, external data sources, and alerts. To open the architect web application, you need to perform the following steps:

1. In an IE browser, enter the BAM start page URL, which is
   `http://<hostname>:<port>/OracleBAM`. The URL is case sensitive.

   If this is the first time that you are accessing the start page, it will redirect you to the login page.

2. Enter the correct username and password, then click on `Go`. For example, you can use the default WebLogic username here to log in.

3. The BAM start page appears, and shows four buttons: **Active Viewer**, **Active Studio**, **Architect**, and **Administrator**.

4. Click on **Architect**. The **BAM Architect** web application launches in a separate web browser window, as shown in the following screenshot:

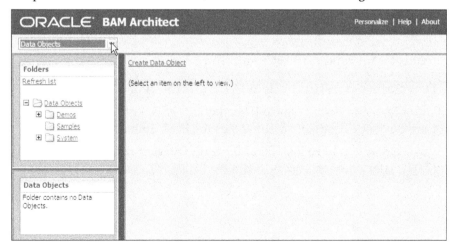

To access the **BAM Architect** web application, you need to log in as a user with the **Administrator** or **Report Architect Application** role. If you see some buttons grayed out in the BAM start page, then the most likely cause is that the user is not granted the corresponding roles to access one of these applications. By default, the WebLogic user defined in the enterprise LDAP server is mapped to the Administrator Application Role, which has the privileges to access all BAM web applications. We are not going to cover Application Roles and their privileges in this section, as you will see more discussion about this topic in *Chapter 6, Managing BAM Securities*.

Creating subfolders

BAM Data Objects are organized in a hierarchy of subfolders, which are internally maintained by BAM Active Data Cache. As you saw in the previous screenshot, the **Data Objects** folder is the root folder that includes the following subfolders:

- **Demos**: A folder that contains four subfolders holding Data Objects for demo reports:
    - ○ **Call Center**: A folder that contains Data Objects used by the **Call Center** report, to demonstrate a call center scenario, where calls are routed, based on the status of various products
    - ○ **Foreign Exchange**: A folder that contains Data Objects used by the **Foreign Exchange** report, to demonstrate the capability to monitor foreign currency trades, the SLA violations, and running totals
    - ○ **Order Booking**: A folder that contains Data Objects used by the **Order Booking** report, to demonstrate the ability to monitor order processing at various stages
    - ○ **Portfolios**: A folder that contains Data Objects used by the **Portfolios** report, which allows users to track changes in stock portfolios

- **Samples**: A folder that contains Data Object samples, which are used throughout the Oracle BAM documentation for demonstrating product features.

- **System**: A folder that contains BAM internal Data Objects. The **History** Data Object is used to track the event histories.

To create a new subfolder, perform the following actions:

1. Click on a folder name in the **Folders** pane, then click on the **Create subfolder** link.

2. Enter a name for the **subfolder**.

3. Click on the **Create folder** button, and a confirmation message appears to indicate the outcome of the action.

The sample Data Objects used in this book are located in the **BookstoreDemo** folder. If you have installed the samples successfully, you should be able to see the folder in the **Folders** pane.

 It is highly recommended to use subfolders to group related Data Objects. The benefit of this best practice is that you can import or export a group of Data Objects, together, by importing or exporting the entire folder.

Data Object design considerations

Data Objects are the key building blocks of your BAM application. Like the concept of XML schemas or database schemas, BAM Data Objects are the schemas for BAM data models that define the structure of the data.

Before making a decision on the design of the Data Objects for your BAM applications, you should consider the following key points:

- Should we define the Data Object as internal or external?
- What fields should we add to the Data Object?
- What field types should we use?

And the recommendations for designing Data Objects are as follows:

- In most cases, you should use internal Data Objects versus external Data Objects. External Data Objects are not directly managed by Active Data Cache, so the real-time data changes are not captured and pushed to the client. Thus, in the case of a real-time dashboard, using external Data Objects as the main data source is not appropriate.

- When defining the data fields for a Data Object, you should consider adding more fields that might be used in the current or future reports. If more data fields are needed in the future, consider creating a new version of the Data Object, instead of editing the original Data Object. Therefore, a new report can be built using the new Data Object, without impacting your existing reports.

- It is a best practice to define the Data Object fields using the same type as in the upstream application. For example, the order shipment date with the type of DateTime in the order management system should have a corresponding field in the BAM Data Object, that is, of the type DateTime. This can prevent expensive data conversion operations when moving data to BAM Active Data Cache.

- Minimize the usage of the lookup fields and calculated fields, as it may introduce performance overhead, given the complexity of the underlying SQL queries.

- Creating indexes for Data Objects may improve the performance of Data Objects queries and report rendering. For example, if you want to filter the Data Objects query result in a report, then creating indexes on the filtering criteria may improve the report rendering performance.

Understanding the mappings between Data Objects and internal database tables

All internally managed Data Objects are persistent to database tables of a **Relational Database Management System (RDBMS)**. BAM 11g R1 certified RDBMSs are Oracle Database, IBM DB2, or Microsoft SQL server. The Data Object persistence store is also called **dataset** in BAM. The dataset name is derived from the Data Object name, plus an underscore prefix. For example, the dataset name for Employees Data Object is _Employees.

The rules for mapping the Data Object field types to dataset column types vary for different repository types. For example, the String field type is mapped to VARCHAR2 in Oracle database, while the corresponding column type Microsoft SQL server is VARCHAR. The following table describes Data Object field types, as well as their column types mapping in the Oracle database:

Field type	Descriptions	Column type In Oracle database
String	A set of characters	VARCHAR2 field is used if 0 < {number of characters <= 2000. CLOB is used otherwise.
Integer	A signed integer ranging from -2,147,483,648 to 2,147,483,647	NUMBER(10,0)
Float	A floating point number	BINARY_DOUBLE: A 64-bit floating point number.
Decimal	Fixed-point NUMBER with maximum precision of 38 decimal digits	NUMBER(38,scale) You need to specify the scale when defining Data Object fields with Decimal type.
Boolean	true or false	NUMBER(1,0) 1 and 0 to represent true and false respectively.
Auto-incrementing integer	Automatically incremented integer starting from 1	NUMBER(19,0)
DateTime	Date and time	Timestamp(6)
Timestamp	Date and time	Timestamp(6)
Calculated	Field type depends on the calculation expression	N/A

Tips for using DateTime **versus** Timestamp

Both DateTime and Timestamp are mapped to Timestamp(6) in the database. The only difference is that you are only allowed to create one Timestamp field in one Data Object, while you can create multiple DataTime fields in the same Data Object.

Creating your first Data Object using BAM Architect

Data Objects are created in the BAM Architect web application. Below are the steps to define a Data Object:

1. In the BAM Architect web application, click on **Data Objects**, or any subfolders in the **Folders** pane.

2. Click on **Create Data Object**.

3. Enter the following details:

   ° **Name for new Data Object**: Enter a name, which can contain strings, numbers, or symbols such as – (dash) and _ (underscore). However, no single or double quotation marks are allowed here.

   ° **Location for new Data Object**: Click on **Browse** to select the subfolder for the location.

   ° **Tip text**: Enter a tip text. This is optional.

   ° **Description**: Enter a description. This is optional.

   ° **External Data Object**: Keep the checkbox unselected.

4. Click on **Add a field** to define data fields for a Data Object.

5. Click on **Create Data Object** to save the Data Object.

A sample Data Object called `Order` is used throughout this book. Now you need to create the `Order` Data Object. The layout is shown in the following screenshot. If you do not want to create this Data Object on your own, you may choose to import the Data Object definition and sample contents using `ICommand`, which will be discussed in the *Using ICommand to import Data Objects* section.

Field	Type	Size/Scale	Nullable	Public
OrderID	Decimal	Scale: 0	Not nullable	☑ Public
OrderDate	DateTime		Nullable	☑ Public
OrderShippedDate	DateTime		Nullable	☑ Public
OrderStatusCode	String	Max size: 30	Nullable	☑ Public
OrderTotal	Decimal	Scale: 2	Nullable	☑ Public
CustomerID	Decimal	Scale: 0	Nullable	☑ Public
OrderReceivedDate	DateTime		Nullable	☑ Public
OrderProcessedDate	DateTime		Nullable	☑ Public

Extending your Data Object with calculated fields

In this section, you will extend the `Order` Data Object with calculated fields. **Calculated fields** are Data Object fields that are derived from other fields, using formulas or calculations. For example, to create a field that represents the order processing time, you can use the following formula:

```
IF ((OrderProcessedDate==NULL) || (OrderReceivedDate==NULL))
    THEN (0)
ELSE ((OrderProcessedDate - OrderReceivedDate)/3600)
```

This formula uses the `IF-THEN-ELSE` expression that calculates the order processing time, and then assigns the result to a calculated field of a Data Object.

To add a calculated field to the `Order` Data Object, perform the following steps:

1. Click on the `Order` Data Object in the `BookstoreDemo` folder.
2. Click on **Layout**, and then click on **Edit Layout**.
3. Click on **Add**.
4. Specify the field name, and then select **Calculation** as the field type.
5. Enter an expression, and click on **Save changes**.

BAM provides a list of operators and expressions, out of the box, which can be used to build calculations for calculated fields. For details about operators and expressions, refer to the *Oracle Fusion Middleware User's Guide for Oracle Business Activity Monitoring 11g Release 1 (11.1.1.6.0)*, which can be accessed at the following URL:

`http://docs.oracle.com/cd/E23943_01/user.1111/e10230/toc.htm`.

Extending your Data Object with lookup fields

In the `Order` Data Object that you saw earlier, we added a field called `OrderStatusCode`, which represents the code for order status. Now, we need a separate field to represent order status description, which is called a **lookup field**. The content of a lookup field is determined through lookups from other Data Objects.

In this section, you will learn how lookup works, and how to add lookup fields in Data Objects.

Understanding how lookup works in BAM

To understand how lookup works, let's take a look at an SQL example, which uses the OUTER JOIN clause to combine records from two tables in a database.

Suppose that we have two tables, ORDER and ORDER_STATUS, as follows:

Table 1: ORDER

ORDERID	ORDERSTATUSCODE
1000	PICK
1001	COMPLETE

Table 2: ORDER_STATUS

ORDERSTATUSCODE	ORDERSTATUS
PICK	Order is being picked
SHIP	Order is being shipped
CANCEL	Order was canceled

To combine the records from these two tables, while keeping all the records from the FOD_ORDER table, we use LEFT OUTER JOIN to build an SQL query, as follows:

```
SELECT orderid, order.orderstatuscode, orderstatus
FROM order
LEFT OUTER JOIN order_status
ON order.orderstatuscode=order_status.orderstatuscode
```

The result returns all the values from the left table (ORDER), plus matched values from the right table (ORDER_STATUS), or NULL, in the case of no matching join predicate.

ORDERID	ORDERSTATUSCODE	ORDERSTATUS
1000	PICK	Order is being picked
1001	COMPLETE	NULL

Lookup in BAM follows the same rule as LEFT OUTER JOIN in SQL. In the Data Objects lookup scenario, the following Data Objects become involved:

- this **Data Object**: A Data Object in which lookup fields are defined. For example, FOD_Order is this Data Object.

- Lookup **Data Object**: A Data Object that contains the source of data for lookup. For example, FOD_Order_Status is a lookup Data Object.

To populate a value from a `lookup` Data Object into a field in `this` Data Object, BAM Active Data Cache builds an SQL query using LEFT OUTER JOIN; the pseudo code is as follows:

```
SELECT dataset1.<data fields>, dataset2.<data fields>
FROM dataset1 LEFT OUTER JOIN dataset2
ON dataset1.field<n>=dataset2.field<n>
```

The FROM clause specifies the joining tables:

- `dataset1` represents the database table for the `this` Data Object
- `dataset2` represents the database table for the `Lookup` Data Object

The ON clause specifies matching conditions for the LEFT OUTER JOIN operation. You can add multiple matching rules, if needed.

The SELECT clause specifies the column names for the result set. When building the queries, all the fields from the `this` Data Object and the `Lookup` Data Object are included in the SELECT clause.

Creating a lookup Data Object

Creating a `Lookup` Data Object is exactly the same as creating a normal Data Object. However, you must not add any lookup fields into `Lookup` Data Objects. In other words, the layout of `Lookup` Data Objects can only contain data fields and calculated fields. The reason is that BAM only supports a one-level lookup (also known as the star schema, for example, `A lookup B`), and does not support multi-level lookups (`A lookup B lookup C`).

 BAM Active Data Cache uses the LEFT OUTER JOIN to combine records from two Data Objects. The query result set includes all the fields from the `Lookup` Data Object. It is a best practice to create a `Lookup` Data Object that contains fields, which are only required for the lookup operations.

Adding lookup fields in Data Objects

Perform the following steps to add a lookup field into the `Order` Data Object:

1. Click on the `Order` Data Object in the BAM Architect.
2. Click on **Layout** to view the layout.
3. Click on **Edit Layout** to edit the layout.

4. Click on **Add one or more lookup fields** at the bottom.

5. In the **Define Lookup Field** dialog box, do the following:

    ◦   Select a **Lookup Data Object**.

    ◦   Specify the **Lookup Field** from the **Lookup Data Object**.

    ◦   Specify matching fields from this Data Object and **Lookup Data Object**. Click on **Add** to add a matching field.

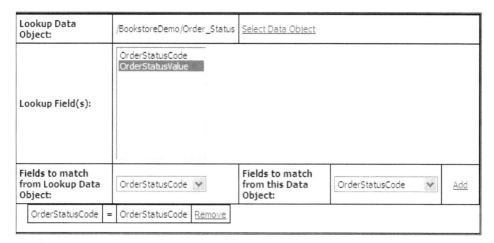

6. Click on **OK** to continue.

7. Click on **Save changes**.

Keep in mind that the Lookup Data Object is based on LEFT OUTER JOIN in SQL. When specifying the Fields to match from the Lookup Data Object, ensure that the fields selected can uniquely identify one record in the Lookup Data Object.

Using external Data Objects

All Data Objects that we created, so far, have been internal Data Objects. But there are some cases in which business data cannot be moved into BAM. It could be due to either the large size of the data, or that we are only granted the **read** permission to use the data. So, we need such a Data Object, called **External Data Object**, that allows us to manage only its layout, but not the contents.

In this section, you will learn how to create an external data source and external Data Object.

Creating external data sources

An **External Data Source (EDS)** is a connection configuration to an external database. It is used by Oracle BAM Active Data Cache to retrieve a table definition and contents from an external database.

To create an external data source, follow these steps:

1. Select **External Data Sources** from the **BAM Architect** drop-down list.
2. Click on **Create**.
3. Enter the database connection details:
    ◦ **External Data Source Name**: Enter a name for the EDS.
    ◦ **Description**: Enter a description.
    ◦ **Driver**: Keep the default value if using the Oracle database. Enter the JDBC driver name for other databases.
    ◦ **Login**: Enter the username.
    ◦ **Password**: Enter the password.
    ◦ **Connection String**: Enter a connection string for the database. For example, `jdbc:oracle:thin:@localhost:1521:orcl`.

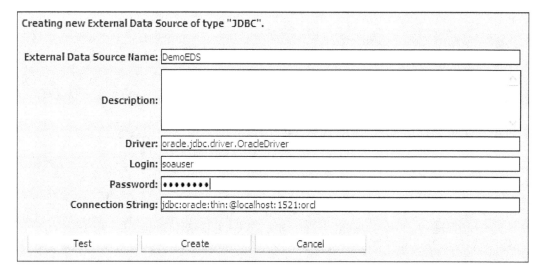

4. Click on **Test** to verify the configuration.
5. Click on **Create** to save the configuration.

Creating external Data Objects

As highlighted in the following screenshot, when creating an external Data Object, you need to execute the following steps:

1. Check the **External Data Object** checkbox.

2. Choose an **External Data Source** from the list.

3. Choose one database table as the data source.

4. Click on **Add a field** or **Add all fields** to define data fields.

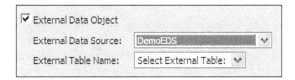

Tips for using external Data Objects

As the contents of external Data Objects are not persistent in the BAM repository, you can only view the contents, but cannot perform insert, update, upsert, or delete operations on the Data Object in BAM Architect web application. In addition, since external Data Objects contents are not directly managed by BAM Active Data Cache, no Active Data will be generated and pushed to the client in the event of data changes in external Data Objects.

Therefore, it is a best practice to avoid using external Data Objects in a real-time report scenario, unless it is used as a Lookup Data Object.

Using ICommand to import Data Objects

ICommand is a command-line utility that can be used to manage BAM artifacts (for example, folders, reports, Data Objects, alerts, and so on), by interacting with BAM Active Data Cache. In this section, you will learn how to use ICommand to import Data Objects.

Configuring ICommand

When BAM ICommand gets executed, it looks for BAM server configuration details in BAMICommandConfig.xml, which is located in the SOA_HOME/bam/config directory. In this URL, SOA_HOME is the home directory for SOA, which is specified during product installation.

To configure ICommand, you need to modify the following two properties in
`BAMICommandConfig.xml`:

- `ADCServerName`: This is the BAM server hostname. You can use `localhost`
  as the server name, if ICommand gets executed in the same host as the
  BAM server.

- `ADCServerPort`: This is the BAM server listening port. By default, it is `9001`.
  If you have changed the listening port at BAM server side, then this property
  needs to be changed accordingly.

> Optionally, you can configure default security credentials
> used by ICommand, so that you will not be prompted to
> enter the username and thw password when ICommand
> is being executed. To configure the default username and
> password, you need to set `ICommand_Default_User_`
> `Name` and `ICommand_Default_Password` properties in
> `BAMICommandConfig.xml`. Note that the password here is in
> clear text, and will be encrypted and replaced during the first
> time you start ICommand.

An example of the configuration looks as follows:

```
<ADCServerName>localhost</ADCServerName>
<ADCServerPort>9001</ADCServerPort>
<ICommand_Default_User_Name>user</ICommand_Default_User_Name>
<ICommand_Default_Password>passwd</ICommand_Default_Password>
```

Setting up environment variables

Before running ICommand, you need to set the `JAVA_HOME` environment variable
as follows :

On Windows OS:

`set JAVA_HOME=<JDK DIR>`

On UNIX/Linux OS:

`export JAVA_HOME=<JDK DIR>`

Running ICommand

To import Data Objects using ICommand, enter the following command in a terminal:

On Windows OS:

```
SOA_HOME/bam/bin/icommand.bat -CMD IMPORT -FILE <file name>
```

On Unix/Linux OS:

```
SOA_HOME/bam/bin/icommand -CMD IMPORT -FILE <file name>
```

To import the sample Data Objects for this book, replace <file name> with SampleDOs.xml that contains the layout and contents of all sample Data Objects. Note that you need to enter the full path for the export file, unless the file is located in the current directory where you run ICommand.

Building your first report

A BAM report contains one or more graphical Views (for example, lists, charts, and key process indicators), rendered in a web browser for displaying high volumes of business data in real time. BAM reports are designed and implemented in the BAM Active Studio web application that provides a variety of template layouts and multiple Views. In this section, you will learn how to build a simple report using the 3D bar chart View in the BAM Active Studio. Creating reports normally includes the following steps:

1. Choosing the Data Object.
2. Choosing data fields.
3. Editing advanced data manipulation properties, such as filtering.
4. Editing View properties.

Creating your first report using the 3D bar chart View

This section explains how to create a simple report using the 3D bar chart template and the /BookstoreDemo/Order Data Object. The layout of the Data Object is described in the previous section.

To create a new report using the 3D bar chart View, perform the following steps:

1. Open the Oracle BAM start page, `http://<hostname>:<port>/OracleBAM` in your IE browser.

2. Click on **Active Studio**. The Oracle BAM Active Studio opens in a new browser window.

3. Click on **Create A New Report** in the left pane. The layout page opens.

4. Click on **Single tiled Report**.

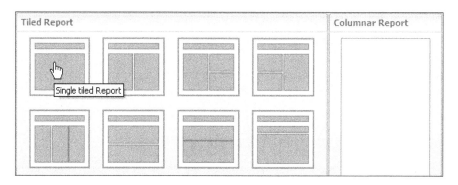

5. A View template opens in the BAM Active Studio. Scroll down through the different View types, and click the 3D bar chart View from the template.

6. A 3D bar chart preview opens in the template, and the View editor opens at the bottom of the page. In the View editor, the first step is to choose the Data Object. Go to the `BookstoreDemo` folder, and then select the `Order` Data Object.

7. Click on **Next**.

8. In the **Choose Data Fields** section, do the following:

   ° **Group By**: Select **OrderStatusCode**

   ° **Chart Values**: Select **OrderID**

   ° **Summary Function(s)**: Select **Count**

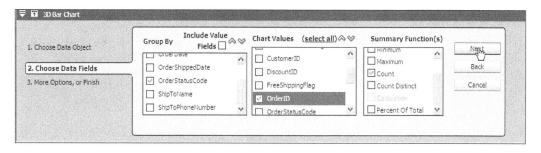

9. Click on **Next**.

10. Click on **Finish**. A 3D bar chart View is displayed with the data.

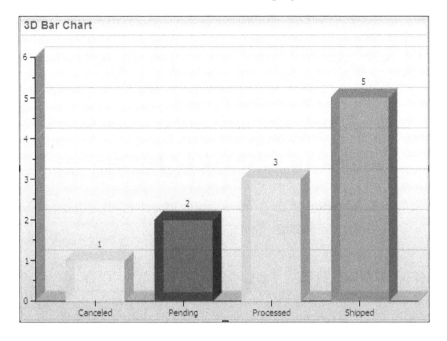

11. Click on **Save Report**.

12. In the dialog-box, create a folder named `BookstoreDemo` in **Shared Report**, if it does not exist, and then save the report in this folder.

> To create a report, you can choose either the **Tiled Report** template or the **Columnar Report** template. The **Tiled Report** template is used for designing graphical Views, such as charts, lists, KPIs, and so on. Various layouts are available here for displaying multiple Views in one page. The **Columnar Report** template is used to produce a View that groups information into sections and displays continuously. You will see more report samples in *Chapter 4, Designing BAM Reports*.

Editing View properties

You can change the report tile, its look and feel, data format, and so on, by editing the properties of a report View. In this section, you will learn how to set the report title and apply a new theme by editing the 3D bar chart View properties.

The following are the steps to edit these View properties:

1. Click the report name you just created in the `BookstoreDemo` folder. A 3D bar chart View opens for editing.

2. Click on **Edit** in the **Actions** pane.

3. Click on **Edit View** in the **View Tasks/Options** pane. A View editor opens at the bottom of the browser.

4. Click on **Properties** to view the **General** tab.

5. In the **View Title** field, enter `Sales Orders By Status`. This will replace the default chart title with a descriptive name.

6. Click on the **Theme** tab, and select any chart theme here.

7. Click on OK, and view the changes.

8. Click on **Save Report** in the **Actions** pane. The changes will then be saved.

9. Click on **Close** to close the report.

Viewing your first report

The easiest way to view a report is using the BAM Active Viewer web application. You can perform the following operations in the BAM Active Viewer:

- **Click on Select Report**: In the **Select a Report** web dialog-box, you can browse and open a report.

- **Click on Print Preview**: In the new web browser window, you can choose to print the report or close the window.

- **Click on Personalize**: In the **Personalize** web dialog-box, you can modify the report loading indicator, time zone preferences, and printing setups.

- **Click on Reprompt**: It is used to reload a report. You will be prompted to choose values, if surface prompts are configured to filter report data.

- **Click on Save Offline**: It is used to save a Snapshot of a report. Note that the offline report cannot process Active Data.

Instead of using Oracle BAM Active Viewer, you can view reports directly in your IE browser. Note that only IE is supported for report rendering in the current BAM release. To view a report in the IE browser, follow these steps:

1. Open a report in Oracle BAM Active Studio.

2. Click on **Copy Shortcut** in the **Actions** pane. A **Copy Shortcut** web page dialog-box opens with the report URL.

3. Copy the URL, and paste it in a new IE browser.

Since every BAM report has a unique URL, you can also include your BAM reports in your existing web application using `iframe`.

Suppose the report URL is as follows:

```
http://<BAMHOST1>:9001/OracleBAM/reportserver/default.jsp?Event=viewR
eport&ReportDef=60&Buttons=False&ReportParameters=()
```

You can add the URL into the `src` attribute of the `iframe` tag. Here is an example:

```
<iframe src
  ="http://<BAMHOST1>:9001/OracleBAM/reportserver/default.jsp?
  Event=viewReport&ReportDef=60&Buttons=False&ReportParameters=()"
  width="100%" height="100%">
</iframe>
```

Summary

In this chapter, you gained some experience with BAM application development, by completing your first Data Object and report design. As you saw earlier, we used ICommand to manually import sample data into Data Objects. However, in the real world, business data needs to be fed into BAM in real time.

In the next chapter, you will learn how to feed business data into BAM. We will compare the different approaches, and provide best practices for doing this.

3
Populating Data Objects with Real-time Data

As you saw in the previous chapter, Data Objects contain the data layout and content on which BAM reports are generated. To render a dynamic report that displays a continuous stream of business data from various data sources (BPEL processes, SOA composites, JMS destinations, web services, and so on), you need to find a solution on populating these Data Objects with real-time business data.

In this chapter, various technologies that can be used to move business data to BAM will be covered:

- Using the Oracle BAM Adapter
- Using BPEL sensors
- Using Enterprise Message Sources
- Using Oracle BAM Web services

Each section in the chapter discusses different technologies, which are not directly related to each other, and may require different skill sets or backgrounds to understand the concepts. So, you may either read these sections one by one, or pick up any section that you are interested in to start with. For example, learning about the Oracle BAM Adapter and BPEL sensors requires an Oracle SOA background. You may skip these two sections completely, and get back to them, if you decide to brush up on these skills later.

Using the Oracle BAM Adapter

In this section, you will learn how to use the Oracle BAM Adapter to populate BAM Data Objects.

The Oracle BAM Adapter is a **Java Connector Architecture (JCA)**-based adapter, which exposes BAM Data Object operations as web services interfaces, by implementing JCA contracts (lifecycle management, security, transactions, and so on). The following is the high level architecture of the BAM Adapter:

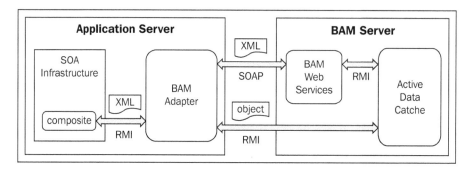

By default, the Oracle BAM Adapter is running on the **Application Server** that hosts the **SOA Infrastructure** (the SOA server), not on the **Application Server** that hosts BAM components. The **BAM Adapter** is primarily referenced in SOA composites as an external service, and its clients can be BPEL processes, Mediator, or OSB components.

The following depicts the typical message flow when performing an operation (`Insert`, `Update`, `Upsert`, or `Delete`) on BAM Active Data Cache through the BAM Adapter:

1. An SOA composite sends an XML payload to the Oracle BAM Adapter over the RMI protocol.

2. The BAM Adapter converts the incoming XML payload to an appropriate format (Java object or XML).

3. If the RMI is specified for communication between the BAM Adapter and the BAM Server, then it invokes the BAM Active Data Cache API directly through RMI.

4. If the SOAP is specified, the BAM Adapter sends a SOAP request to the BAM Web Service interface, which in turn invokes the Active Data Cache API.

Configuring the Oracle BAM Adapter

In order to use the Oracle BAM Adapter in SOA composites, you need to configure the Oracle BAM Adapter in the WebLogic Server console as follows:

1. Enter the Oracle WebLogic Server console URL (`http://<hostname>:7001/console`) in a web browser. Log in using the users with administrator roles, such as `weblogic`.

2. In the **Domain Structure** pane, click on `Deployments`.

3. In the **Deployments** table, find and click on **OracleBamAdapter** in the **Name** column.

4. Click on the `Configuration` tab and **Outbound Connection Pools** sub tab.

5. In the **Outbound Connection Pool Configuration Table**, expand **oracle.bam. adapter.adc.RMIConnectionFactory**, and click on `eis/bam/rmi`, which is the JNDI location for the RMI connection factory.

6. In the **Outbound Connection Properties** table, enter the following values:

    ○ **HostName**: Enter a BAM Server hostname.

    ○ **PortNumber**: Specify the BAM Server listening port. The default port is `9001`.

    ○ **InstanceName**: Specify the BAM instance name. Keep the default as `ADCServer1`.

    ○ **UserName**: Enter the username, which is granted the BAM Administrator role. You can use `weblogic` user here.

    ○ **Password**: Enter the password.

    Make sure that you press `Enter` after setting each value. Click on **Save**.

7. Create a new directory, and save the deployment plan (`Plan.xml`) in the new directory.

8. You need to update your deployment to reflect the changes. Go to the **Deployments** page again, select the checkbox for **OracleBamAdapter**, and click on **Update**.

9. Click on **Finish** to finish updating the deployment for the Oracle BAM Adapter.

The Oracle BAM Adapter can either use the RMI or the SOAP communication protocols to connect to an Oracle BAM Server. As shown in the following table, you need to configure the **eis/bam/rmi** instance for using RMI protocol, while configuring the `eis/bam/soap` instance for SOAP communications:

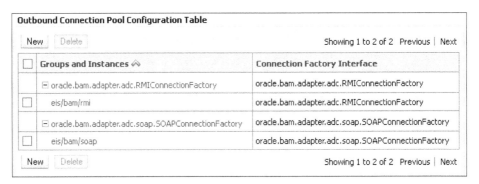

As shown in the BAM Adapter architecture diagram, when connecting to an Oracle BAM Server through the RMI protocol, the Oracle BAM Adapter internally invokes the BAM Active Data Cache Session Bean interface through a remote EJB call, and while using SOAP, it calls the `DataObjectOperationsByID` webservice API, which in turn invokes the BAM Active Data Cache APIs. So, the RMI protocol gives you a better performance and transactional support. You should consider the RMI protocol as the preferred option. The BAM Adapter also provides you a second option (the SOAP protocol), which can be used in a scenario where SOAP communication is the only way to connect to the BAM Server. For example, suppose that the remote BAM server is behind a firewall through which RMI traffic is not allowed. In this case, SOAP would be the only option.

When clicking on **Save** in the WebLogic Server console, to save the Oracle BAM Adapter configuration changes, it only writes the changes to the deployment plan represented by `plan.xml`. To make the changes take effect, you need to update the adapter, which simply redeploys the adapter using the deployment plan. In an **high availability** (**HA**) environment, this file should be stored in a shared disk, which is the best practice.

Using the Oracle BAM Adapter in SOA composites

In this section, we will use a sample SOA composite (`PopulateDOComposite`) to demonstrate how to send business data to Data Objects through the Oracle BAM Adapter.

Creating a BAM Server connection

To create a BAM Server connection in **JDeveloper**, perform the following steps:

1. Open the SOA sample application in JDeveloper.
2. In the **Application Resources** pane, right click on **Connections**, then click on **New Connection | BAM...** to open the **BAM Connection Wizard**.

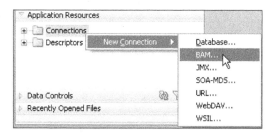

3. In the **BAM Connection Wizard Step 1 of 3** screen, select **Application Resources**, and enter a name for the connection. Click on **Next**.

4. In the **BAM Connection Wizard Step 2 of 3** screen, enter the following details:

    ○   **BAM Web Host:** Enter the hostname of the WebLogic Server (the Managed Server for BAM) to which the BAM Web applications and report server are deployed.

    ○   **HTTP Port:** Enter the HTTP listen port of the Managed Server for BAM. The default value is 9001.

    ○   **BAM Server Host:** Enter the name of the host to which the BAM Server components (Active Data Cache, Report Cache, and Event Engine) are deployed. In a single node environment, the hostname of the BAM Server should be the same as the BAM Web.

    ○   **JNDI Port:** Enter the RMI Port, which is used to connect to BAM Active Data Cache on the BAM Server. By default, this port is the same as the HTTP Port on the BAM Server.

    ○   **User Name:** Enter the username, which is granted the BAM Administrator role. You can use weblogic user.

    ○   **Password:** Enter the password.

5. In the **BAM Connection Wizard Step 3 of 3** screen, click on **Test Connection** to test the HTTP connection, JNDI connection, and Data Object browsing. Click on **Next**, if the test is successful.

6. Click on **Finish**. In the **Resource Palette** pane, the new BAM Server connection is listed under the BAM node in the **IDE Connections** section.

A BAM Server connection can be either created in the **Resource Palette** or in the **Application Resources**. BAM Server connections in the **Resource Palette** are IDE-level resources, which can be used by all applications, while the connections in the **Application Resources** are in the application scope, and thus are only visible to the application itself. Currently, the Oracle BAM Adapter Configuration Wizard can only use application-scoped BAM Server connections, so you should not create BAM Server connections in the **Resource Palette**.

Using the Oracle BAM Adapter in an SOA composite

The Oracle BAM Adapter is an external service from an SOA composite perspective. In order to invoke operations exposed by the Oracle BAM Adapter, you need to create an external reference, which acts as a wrapper to the Oracle BAM Adapter, based on the **Service Component Architecture (SCA)** standard.

According to the SCA standard, creating an external reference to the Oracle BAM Adapter internally, creates the following files in the SOA composite project:

- `.wsdl` **file**: This is a WSDL file that defines the interface for the external reference.
- `.xsd` **file**: This is an XML schema file that is created, based on the Oracle BAM Data Object definition.
- `.jca` **file**: This is a JCA binding configuration file

The Oracle JDeveloper IDE provides a GUI-based wizard to facilitate the creation of SCA references. To create an external reference for the Oracle BAM Adapter, perform the following steps:

1. Double-click on `composite.xml` in the SOA project. The SOA composite design view appears.

2. In the SOA composite view, right-click on the area in the **External References** pane, and then select **Insert… | BAM Adapter**. The **BAM Adapter Configuration Wizard** appears. Click on **Next**.

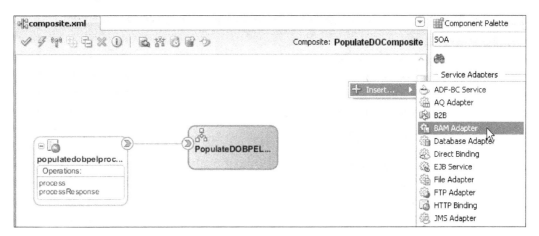

3. In **Step 2 of 5**, enter a service name (for example, `WriteToBAMService`), and click on **Next**.

4. In **Step 3 of 5**, enter the following details:

   ○ **Data Object**: Select the `/BookstoreDemo/Order_Status` Data Object.

   ○ **Operation**: Choose one operation (for example, **Insert**).

   ○ **Operation Name**: Enter an operation name.

   ○ **Keys**: This is optional. Specify the primary keys for the Data Object, if the operation is **Update**, **Upsert**, or **Delete**.

5. Click on **Next**.

6. In **Step 4 of 5**, specify the JNDI name for the Oracle BAM Adapter. Use `eis/ bam/rmi` that you configured earlier in the WebLogic Server console.

7. Click on **Next**.

8. In **Step 5 of 5**, click on **Finish**. An external reference for the Oracle BAM Adapter is created, and appears in the SOA composite design view as shown in the following screenshot:

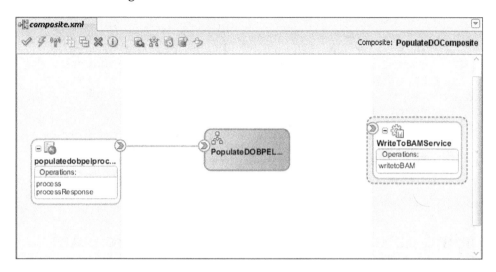

The Insert operation may produce duplicate records in the Data Objects, as it does not contain the **primary key (PK)** constraint. You cannot specify PKs for Insert operations, which may produce duplicate records in the Data Objects. If you want to avoid data duplication, try to use the Upsert operation that combines the functionality of Insert and Update.

Now you can see that .wsdl, .xsd, and .jca files are present in the SOA composite project folder. Let's take a closer look at the .jca, file, which is shown as follows:

```
<adapter-config name="WriteToBAMService" adapter="BAM Adapter" wsdlLocation="WriteToBAMService.wsdl"
   xmlns="http://platform.integration.oracle/blocks/adapter/fw/metadata">
  <connection-factory location="eis/bam/rmi" UIConnectionName="BAMServerConnection2" adapterRef=""/>
  <endpoint-interaction portType="writetoBAM_ptt" operation="writetoBAM">
    <interaction-spec className="oracle.bam.adapter.adc.ADCInteractionSpec">
      <property name="DataObjectName" value="/BookstoreDemo/Order_Status"/>
      <property name="OperationType" value="Upsert"/>
      <property name="InBatch" value="false"/>
      <property name="Keys" value="_OrderStatusCode"/>
    </interaction-spec>
  </endpoint-interaction>
</adapter-config>
```

The highlighted lines in the .jca file are the configuration details for the Oracle BAM Adapter connection factory and Data Object interaction properties, which include DataobjectName, OperationType, InBatch, and Keys.

The property values defined in the .jca file are case-sensitive. For example, /BookstoreDemo/Order_Status is a valid value for the DataObjectName property, but if you change the value to lower case, such as /BookstoreDemo/order_status, the BAM operation will fail during runtime.

Do not modify this file manually, unless you are sure about the values. It is always a best practice to reconfigure the Oracle BAM Adapter, by going through the Oracle BAM Adapter configuration wizard when there are any changes to the backend Oracle BAM Data Object definition.

Sending data to BAM through the Oracle BAM Adapter

Once the external reference to the BAM Adapter is configured, sending data to BAM through the BAM Adapter becomes straightforward.

First of all, you need to wire the SOA component (BPEL or mediator) to the external reference that you defined earlier.

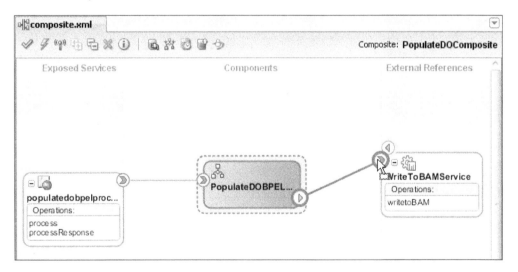

After that, you need to design and implement the SOA component (BPEL or mediator) that acts as the client to the BAM Adapter. The sample composite (PopulateDOComposite) in this book has one BPEL component (The PolulateDOBPELProcess BPEL process), which invokes the BAM Adapter operation through the external reference. Double-click the BPEL component in the composite design view, and the BPEL design view opens as shown in the following screenshot:

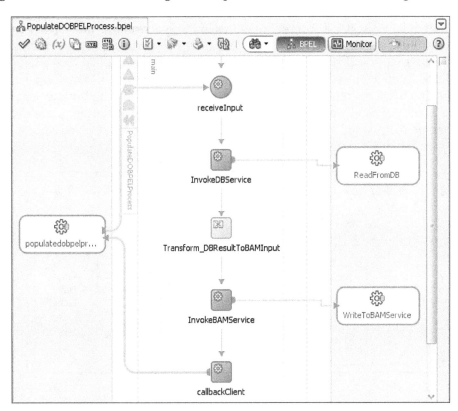

In the BPEL processes, **partner** links represent the WSDL interfaces (outbound or inbound), through which BEPL interacts with external system or services. As illustrated in this screenshot, there are two outbound partner links, **ReadFromDB** and **WriteToBAMService**, which represent the interfaces for the Database Adapter and the BAM Adapter, respectively.

InvokeDBService is an Invoke activity, which is used to query the Order_Status table in the BookstoreDemo schema through the ReadFromDB partner link, and the BPEL InvokeBAMService activity is used to invoke operations exposed through the Oracle BAM Adapter. The Transform activity is used to initialize the BAM Adapter input variable, by using XSL to transform the Database Adapter query result into an XML format.

As the design and implementation of SOA composites is beyond the scope of this book, we only discussed an overview of using the BAM Adapter in a SOA composite in this section. To learn more about SOA development, refer to Oracle SOA documentation or SOA development books available on the market.

Enabling batching

By default, the Oracle BAM Adapter operates in the synchronous mode (non-batching mode). As illustrated in the following diagram, the client thread **T1** that executes the BPEL **Invoke** activity also executes the **BAM Adapter** API, which in turn performs a BAM operation, by invoking the remote API of the BAM Active Data Cache. In this case, the BAM operation is performed synchronously, and the **Invoke** activity in BPEL is blocked and waits for the completion of the BAM Adapter operation. If a BAM Server is down or becomes unavailable, the client (the **Invoke** activity) will be blocked until the JTA transaction time-out occurs.

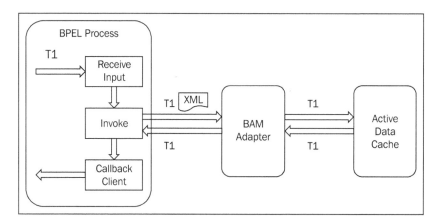

With batching enabled, the BAM Adapter operates in the asynchronous mode. As shown in the following diagram, after the XML payload that contains a BAM operation (Insert, Update, Upsert, or Delete) request, is delivered successfully to the BAM Adapter. The client thread **T1** returns immediately without waiting for the response from the BAM API call. In the meantime, instead of transforming and sending the XML request to the BAM Active Data Cache in real time, the BAM Adapter queues these requests, and sends a number of requests as a batch, until certain conditions are met.

When the BAM Adapter operates in the batching mode, a separate thread (**T2**) is allocated to execute the batching API of the Active Data Cache, which processes all the requests in the same batch, in one transaction. Any failure that occurs in the batch will cause the entire batch operation to be rolled back. Note that BAM Adapter and BAM Active Data Cache only support local JTA transaction.

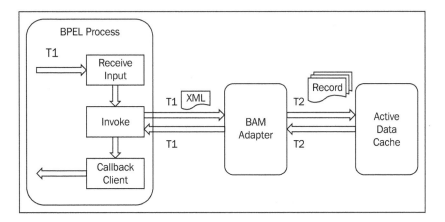

The following are the two major benefits provided by batching:

- **High availability**: If batching is not enabled, in the case of BAM Server crash or outage, the BAM Adapter client code will block, the transaction timeout error will happen at the client side, and the XML payload sent to the Oracle BAM Adapter will be discarded. Batching is particularly useful in this case, as it effectively isolates the Adapter client with the BAM Server by using an asynchronous approach to handle the invocation of the BAM ADC APIs.

- **High performance**: Performance could be improved at both the client side and the BAM Adapter side. The execution of the BAM Adapter client is not blocked by the invocation of the BAM adapter invocation, thus helping reduce the response time for the client. Most importantly, performance improvement can be achieved by reducing the number of remote method invocations and network round trips. Without batching, each XML payload sent by the BAM Adapter client will force the BAM Adapter to place a remote method call to the BAM Active Data Cache API over RMI. With batching, the BAM Adapter sends a batch of records (which are compressed) over the network in one API call to the ADC batching API, which is provided to handle batch processing.

How to enable batching

You can enable batching through the Oracle BAM Adapter configuration wizard, or by simply editing the BAM Adapter .jca file, by setting the InBatch property to true.

```
<property name="InBatch" value="true"/>
```

You need to redeploy the SOA composite to make the change take effect.

Configuring batching properties

You can control the batching behaviors, such as how many records can be included in a batch, and how many batches can be queued up in the Oracle BAM Adapter, by tuning the batching properties as shown in the following table:

Property name	Property type	Description
Batch_Lower_Limit	java.lang. Integer	This is a threshold that represents the minimal number of records in a batch. A batch will be sent to a BAM Server when this threshold is reached. The default value is 1000.
Batch_Timeout	java.lang. Integer	This property represents the elapsed time after the Oracle BAM Adapter operations (Insert, Update, Upsert, and Delete) are invoked. The default value is 5000 in milliseconds.
Batch_Upper_Limit	java.lang. Integer	This property represents the maximum number of records in one batch. The default value is 5000.
Block_On_Batch_ Full	java.lang. Boolean	This property represents a Boolean value that indicates whether the client will block if the last batch is full. The default value is false.
Number_Batches	java.lang. Integer	This property represents the number of batches that are allowed to be queued up before sending to a BAM Server. The default value is 10.

Note that this table only lists the properties used for the RMI communication with a BAM Server. The corresponding properties for the SOAP communication protocol are named with a prefix SOAP_ (for example, SOAP_Batch_Timeout), and have the same meanings and default values.

A batch is sent to a BAM Server, if the elapsed time for invoking the Oracle BAM Adapter operation reaches the Batch_Timeout threshold, or the number of records in the batch reaches the Batch_Lower_Limit threshold. If the last batch in the queue is full, and the Block_On_ Batch_Full is set to false, then all the forthcoming records sent to the BAM Adapter will be discarded.

To configure the Oracle BAM Adapter batching properties, you need to perform the following steps:

1. Click on **OracleBamAdapter** in the **Deployments** table in the WebLogic Server console.

2. Click on the **Configuration** tab and **Properties** sub tab.

3. Set the specific **Batching** properties, and click on **Save**.

4. Go to the **Deployments** page again and select the checkbox for **OracleBamAdapter**, and click on **Update**.

5. Click on **Finish** to finish updating the deployment for the Oracle BAM Adapter.

6. Restart the SOA Server that hosts **OracleBamAdapter**.

Using BPEL sensors

BPEL sensors are used to monitor the specific events throughout the lifecycle of a BPEL instance. The specific event can be the activation or completion of an activity or change of a variable value. When a sensor is triggered, a specific sensor value is created. The sensor value contains the time stamp, the value of the variable at the moment the sensor triggered, and other related information. The data format of the sensor value is in a normalized and well-defined XML format.

Using a BAM Sensor Action

An Oracle BAM Sensor Action is used to publish BPEL sensor data into existing Data Objects on a BAM Server. This is another way that you can integrate from BPEL to BAM.

To create BAM sensor actions, perform the following steps in JDeveloper:

1. Ensure that the BAM Server connection is present in the **Application Resource** pane in JDeveloper. To create a BAM connection, follow the instructions in the *Creating a BAM Server connection* section that you saw earlier.

2. Open a BPEL process in JDeveloper, and select **Monitor** at the top of the BPEL designer to **Change to Monitor view**.

3. Create an activity sensor and a variable sensor in the **Structure** pane:

   ° Expand **Sensors**, then right-click on **Variables | Create**.

   ° An activity sensor can also be created from the activity in the BPEL process. Right-click on the selected activity, and select **Create | Sensor**.

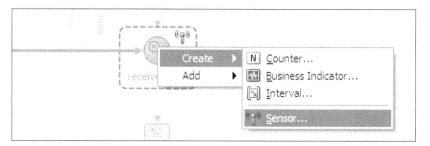

4. In the structure page, right-click on **Sensor Actions**, then click on **Create | BAM Sensor Action**. The **Create Sensor Action** wizard appears.

5. Enter the following details in the wizard:

   ° **Action Name**: Enter an action name.

   ° **Sensor**: Choose a sensor variable as the source.

   ° **Data Object**: Choose a BAM Data object as the target.

   ° **Operation**: Choose a Data Object operation.

   ° **Keys**: Specify the keys for the Data Object if needed.

   ° **Map File**: Specify an XSL file that is used to transform data from the sensor variable to the Data Object.

   ° **BAM Connection Factory JNDI**: Specify the JNDI name for the BAM Adapter connection factory, which can be either **eis/bam/rmi** or **eis/bam/soap**.

   ° **Enable Batching**: Check this option to enable batching. This is the same as the **BAM Adapter Batching** option that you saw earlier.

6. Click on **OK**. The mapping file editor appears. Edit the mapping to transform data from sensor XML payload to XML input for BAM Adapter.

BAM Sensor action invokes the BAM Adapter APIs, which in turn sends the data to the BAM Active Data Cache. So, it reuses the BAM Adapter configuration, such as the JNDI name for the connection factory, batching properties, and so on.

In this chapter, we provide a sample SOA project called `SensorSample` that showcases how to use the BPEL Sensor and Sensor Actions to populate data changes to the BAM Data Object. Follow the instructions from the README file to set up and run the project.

If the variable type is defined inline in the WSDL file, this variable cannot be listed in the **Variable Xpath Builder** window, which is used to add the variable to a variable sensor. Thus, always assign a variable type to an Element or a Message, explicitly, defined in a standalone XSD file.

If the layout of a Data Object changes, you need to restart the BAM server to make the changes take effect at the UI side. Otherwise, you will get a runtime error, which is BAM-06008: The XML payload is invalid; extra contents were found.

Using Enterprise Message Sources

Enterprise Message Sources (**EMS**) provides direct **Java Message Service** (**JMS**) connectivity to the Oracle BAM Server, by mapping messages directly to Oracle BAM Data Objects. Oracle BAM Server can read data directly from any JMS-based message queue or topic through the Messaging Framework.

BAM EMS supports the following JMS Servers or JMS providers:

- WebLogic Server JMS provider
- AQ JMS
- WebSphereMQ
- Tibco
- SonicMQ

In this section, you will learn how to create an EMS to populate the Data Object with messages received from JMS queues on the WebLogic JMS Server.

Creating an EMS

To create an EMS, you need to select **Enterprise Messaging Sources** from the list in the BAM Architect web application, and click on **Create**. In the EMS configuration page, provide details in the following sections:

Configuring JMS Server connection properties

EMS acts as a Java client that connects to the JMS Server to consume messages from JMS destinations (queues or topics). In the JMS programming model, use the **Java Naming and Directory Interface (JNDI)** to find a `javax.jms.ConnectionFactory` object and a `javax.jms.Destination` object. To perform JNDI lookup operations, EMS needs to instantiate a `javax.naming.InitialContext` class, using the following properties:

- `javax.naming.Context.INITIAL_CONTEXT_FACTORY`
- `javax.naming.Context.PROVIDER_URL`
- `javax.naming.Context.SECURITY_PRINCIPAL`
- `javax.naming.Context.SECURITY_CREDENTIALS`

To configure the JMS Server connection details, enter the following details in the UI:

- **Initial Context Factory**: Enter a name that is used to set `javax.naming.Context.INITIAL_CONTEXT_FACTORY`. For Weblogic JMS Provider, enter `weblogic.jndi.WLInitialContextFactory`.

- **JNDI Service Provider URL**: Enter a URL that is used to set `javax.naming.Context.PROVIDER_URL`. For example , the URL of the WebLogic Server JMS provider could be `t3://localhost:9001`.

- **Topic/Queue ConnectionFactory Name**: Enter the JNDI name for `TopicConnectionFactory` or `QueueConnectionFactory`.

- **Topic/Queue Name**: Enter the JNDI name for JMS topic or queue.

- **JNDI Username**: Enter a name that is used to set `javax.naming.Context.SECURITY_PRINCIPAL`.

- **JNDI Password**: Enter the password that is used to set `javax.naming.Context.SECURITY_CREDENTIALS`.

Configuring JMS message consumption properties

In this section, set up the JMS Message consumption-related properties as follows:

- **JMS Message Type**: Select **TextMessage** or **MapMessage**.

- **Durable Subscriber Name (Optional)**: Enter a durable subscriber name. A durable subscription can preserve messages published on a topic while the subscriber is not active.

- **Message Selector (Optional)**: Enter a name-value pair for filtering JMS messages. The name value pair format should be `name=value`. In the current release, only one name-value pair is supported.

The **Message Selector** option allows you to process multiple message types through a single JMS destination. However, you should be careful when using this option for high volume message processing, as it could dramatically impact performance.

Configuring Data Object operation properties

In this section, you specify how to populate BAM Data Object as follows:

- **Data Object Name**: Click on **Browse** to select the Data Object to which EMS sends the data.

- **Operation**: Select a Data Object operation name (`Insert`, `Update`, `Upsert`, or `Delete`).

- **Batching**: Specify whether the EMS communicates with the Oracle BAM Active Data Cache batching API for batch processing.

- **Transaction**: Choose **Yes**, if you want to enable transaction for Messaging batching processing.

 By default, EMS sends individual JMS messages to the BAM Active Data Cache. If batching is enabled, EMS will send a batch of messages to BAM Active Data Cache, which will process it as a unit. As EMS resides in the same EJB container as Active Data Cache, and there is no network traffic between EMS and Active Data Cache, sending a batch of messages does not make much difference than sending one message at a time, in terms of performance.

Configuring other properties

You need to set up the following properties as well:

- **Name**: Enter the name of the EMS

- **Start when BAM Server starts**: Specify whether the EMS should be automatically started after Oracle BAM Server starts

 Every time you apply the changes for EMS configurations, EMS will be stopped automatically. When EMS is at **Stopped** status, it cannot consume any messages. So, you need to restart it manually by clicking on the **Start** link.

A case study

Suppose that we have an inventory system, which will send an XML message containing warehouse stock level information to the WebLogic JMS queue when certain conditions are met. Now, we have a new requirement, which is to use EMS to consume the message from the queue, and invoke BAM Active Data Cache API to persist the data to the /BookstoreDemo/Inventory Data Object.

The following is an example that demonstrates how to configure EMS:

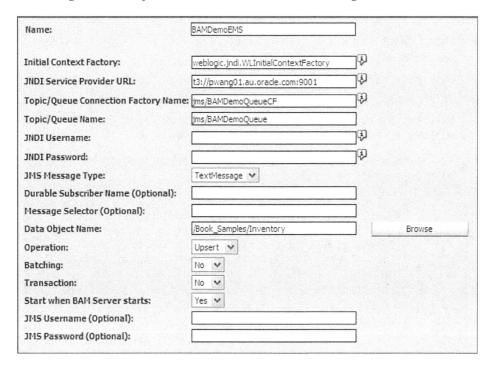

In this configuration, we do not specify the **JNDI Username** and the **JNDI Password**, as InitialContext instantiation does not require these properties when the BAM and the JMS server reside in the same WebLogic Server container.

XML formatting

XML formatting is used to specify how to parse the JMS messages received by EMS, which are in XML format. Enter the following details to configure XML formatting:

- **Pre-Processing**: Check this option, if you want to apply XSL transformation code to pre-process the XML messages consumed by EMS. Instead of the original document, the transformation result is parsed by the XML parser.

- **Message Element Name**: Specify the XML element whose child elements or attributes are the ones used for XML to the Data Object mapping.

- **Column Value**: Choose **Element Tag** if the data are stored in sub elements. Choose **Attribute** if the data are stored in attributes.

 Pre-processing is also required to transform the message consumed from JMS sources from a complex structure (XML elements with hierarchies) to a flat structure (a single level XML fragments) that can then be mapped to Data Object fields. You will see an example in *Chapter 5,* .

Suppose that EMS receives the following messages from a JMS Queue:

```
<Inventory xmlns="http://www.packtpub.com/5443/samples/inventory">
   <ProductID>1</ProductID>
   <WarehouseID>101</WarehouseID>
   <InventoryLevel>200</InventoryLevel>
</Inventory>
```

The **XML Formatting** configuration should look as follows:

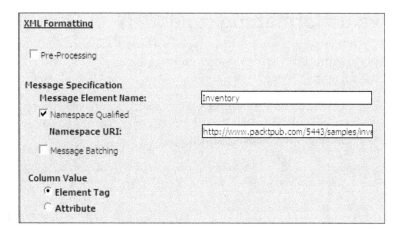

Suppose that the JMS message received by EMS contains a collection of items as follows:

```
<InventoryBatch>
  <Inventory>
    <ProductID>1</ProductID>
    <WarehouseID>101</WarehouseID>
    <InventoryLevel>200</InventoryLevel>
  </Inventory>
  <Inventory>
    <ProductID>2</ProductID>
    <WarehouseID>101</WarehouseID>
    <InventoryLevel>400</InventoryLevel>
  </Inventory>
</InventoryBatch>
```

To parse this XML document, you need to check the **Message Batching** option, and then enter `InventoryBatch` for **Batch Element Name**.

Message Batching is an indicator that tells EMS to parse XML messages, which contain a collection of items. When **Message Batching** is selected, ensure that you also set the **Transaction** property in the basic configuration section to **Yes**, which reinforces transactional behavior when processing a batch of messages.

Note that **Message Batching** is different than the batching property for the BAM Adapter.

Source value formatting (optional)

When the XML data type is `xs:dateTime`, you can skip the source value formatting. This step is only required if XML messages contain `DateTime` values, which are not in `xs:dateTime` format.

To format `DateTime` source values, you need to specify a correct pattern for `java.text.SimpleDateFormat`. For details about `java.text.SimpleDateFormat`, refer to the Java6 API documentation at the following URL:

```
http://download.oracle.com/javase/6/docs/api/java/text/
SimpleDateFormat.html
```

Configuring XML to Data Object mapping

To configure a XML to Data Object mapping, click on **Add** to add a mapping rule. The following is an example of XML to Data Object mapping:

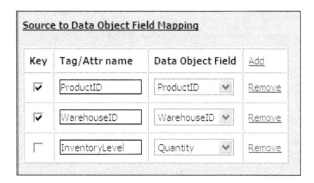

As you can see, the XML elements ProductID, WarehouseID, and Inventorylevel are mapped to the corresponding **Data Object fields**. And ProductID and WarehouseID are selected as **Keys**.

After you complete this section, you can click on **Save** to create the EMS.

Testing EMS

EMS defines the JMS connection, transformation, formatting, and mapping information. To verify the behavior of the EMS you configured, you need to perform testing, which covers end-to-end messaging flow in EMS.

In the BAM Architect web application, you can click on **Test** to perform basic testing, which only tests the connection details to a JMS provider. To verify the transformation, value formatting, mapping, and Data Object operations, you need to perform end-to-end testing, which often involves a JMS client, and, sometimes, a demo report.

Testing EMS Using WebLogic Server console

To use WebLogic Server console as a JMS client to test EMS, perform the following steps:

1. Log in to the WebLogic Server console that hosts the JMS queue/topic that you want to test.

2. In the **Domain Structure** page in the WebLogic Server console, navigate to **Services | Messaging | JMS Modules**.

3. Click on the JMS module and the queue/topic that your EMS connects to.

4. Click on the **Monitoring** tab, and then check the checkbox in front of the queue/topic that you want to test.

5. Click on **Show Messages**.

6. Click on **New**. The **Produce JMS Message** page appears.

7. Provide the XML payload in the **Body** text area. Click on **OK** to produce the message.

8. Verify if the new record is populated into the Data Object in the BAM Architect web application.

For example, suppose that you provide the following XML payload:

```
<Inventory xmlns="http://www.packtpub.com/5443/samples/inventory">
  <ProductID>1</ProductID>
  <WarehouseID>101</WarehouseID>
  <InventoryLevel>200</InventoryLevel>
</Inventory>
```

You can verify the test result by viewing the records in the Data Object. If testing is successful, you should see a record in the Data Object contents view, as shown in the following screenshot:

Row ID	ProductID	WarehouseID	Quantity
11	1	101	200

You can also inspect the statistics for the EMS to verify your test result. If you click on **Metrics** in the EMS page, the **Statistics for Enterprise Message Source** table appears.

 The statistics show the total number of received, committed, and lost messages, based on the rule as follows:
Total Messages Received = Total Messages committed in ADC + Total Messages Lost

If **Total Messages Lost** is zero or unchanged since the previous test, testing is successful; otherwise, testing fails, and JMS messages are lost. This means that BAM received the message, but was unable to process it in the Data Object. A reason for this could be that the message was in an invalid XML format.

Transaction and fault handling

EMS supports the JTA transaction. The Messaging Framework, which handles JMS message consumption, does not propagate JTA transaction to EMS. Thus, EMS always starts a new transaction after a JMS message is delivered to EMS. Therefore, the transaction boundary in BAM is actually between the EMS and the Active Data Cache, and not between the Messaging Framework and the Active Data Cache.

 When there is a fault happening in the message flow from EMS to Active Data Cache, the current transaction rolls back, but only to the point where it is started in EMS. Since JMS message consumption is not a part of this transaction, messages are discarded in the end. Thus, it is highly recommended to use the fault handling mechanism to keep track of the error messages and payloads.

You can handle faults in the following ways:

- Log faulted messages with or without payloads
- Write faulted messages to Data Objects or a separate JMS queue/topic

The following is an example of fault handling in the EMS configuration page:

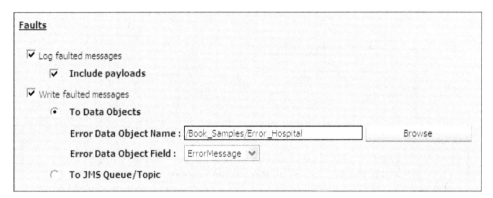

Suppose you send the following payload to a JMS Queue:

```
<Inventory xmlns="http://www.packtpub.com/5443/samples/inventory">
    <ProductID>1</ProductID>
    <WarehouseID>101</WarehouseID>
    <InventoryLevel>Null</InventoryLevel>
</Inventory>
```

As `<InventoryLevel>` contains an invalid value, it causes a transaction rollback. The message is lost in this case. You should be able to see the faulted message and the XML payload in the server's log file, and the `ErrorMessage` field in the `/BookstoreDemo/Error_Hospital` Data Object, as shown in the following screenshot:

```
EMS BAMDemoEMS failed to process the payload:
<Inventory xmlns="http://www.packtpub.com/5443/samples/inventory">
    <ProductID>1</ProductID>
    <WarehouseID>101</WarehouseID>
    <InventoryLevel>Null</InventoryLevel>
</Inventory>
with the following exception:For input string: "Null"
```

Using Oracle BAM Web services

Oracle BAM provides Web services interfaces, which allow clients to interact with BAM server components. In this section, you will learn how to invoke the `DataObjectOperationsByName` Web service to populate data into Data Objects.

DataObjectOperationsByName Web service overview

`DataObjectOperationsByName` is a Web service that can be used to perform Data Object operations (`Insert`, `Update`, `Upsert`, and `Delete`), in which XML payloads are defined using the `Name` attribute.

For example, to insert a record into the `Inventory` Data Object, you can invoke the `DataObjectOperationsByName` Web service, by sending a SOAP request, which contains the following XML payload:

```
<DataObject Name="Inventory" Path="/Book_Samples">
  <Contents>
    <Row>
      <Column Name="ProductID" Value="2"/>
      <Column Name="WarehouseID" Value="101"/>
      <Column Name="Quantity" Value="300"/>
    </Row>
  </Contents>
</DataObject>
```

The payload defines the Data Object name, location, and its contents, which contain a collection of column name-value pairs.

 Do not include lookup columns or calculated columns in the XML payload when invoking the `DataObjectOperationsByName` Web service, as the values for these columns are automatically populated by the BAM Server.

The WSDL location for the `DataObjectOperationsByName` web service is as follows:

`http://<hostname>:<port>/OracleBAMWS/WebServices/DataObjectOperations ByName?WSDL`.

In this URL, `<hostname>` is the BAM Server hostname, and `<port>` is the BAM Server listening port.

 The `DataObjectOperationsByName` Web service is protected with basic authentication. You need to log in as a valid user in the Weblogic Server security realm to invoke the service.

Using the DataObjectOperationsByName web service

You can invoke this web service using any client, by sending a valid SOAP request over HTTP. To demonstrate the usage of the `DataObjectOperationsByName` web service, we use SOAPUI, a web service client used to invoke the service.

Here is a sample SOAP request generated in SOAPUI:

```
<soapenv:Envelope
  xmlns:soapenv="http://schemas.xmlsoap.org/soap/envelope/"
  xmlns:bam="http://xmlns.oracle.com/bam">
  <soapenv:Header/>
  <soapenv:Body>
    <bam:Insert>
      <!--Optional:-->
      <bam:xmlPayload>
        &lt;DataObject Name="Inventory" Path="/Book_Samples"&gt;
          &lt;Contents&gt;
            &lt;Row&gt;
              &lt;Column Name="ProductID" Value="2"/&gt;
              &lt;Column Name="WarehouseID" Value="101"/&gt;
              &lt;Column Name="Quantity" Value="200"/&gt;
            &lt;/Row&gt;
          &lt;/Contents&gt;
        &lt;/DataObject&gt;
      </bam:xmlPayload>
    </bam:Insert>
  </soapenv:Body>
</soapenv:Envelope>
```

As you can see in the highlighted code, all the `<` and `>` characters inside the `<bam:xmlPayload>` are replaced with the escape characters `&lt;` and `&gt;`, respectively. Otherwise, the operation fails. The reason behind this is that the data type for `<bam:xmlPayload>` is `string`, and parsing string type payload containing characters, such as `<` or `>`, will cause a XML parser error.

The result returns an empty `InsertResponse` element, which indicates that the test is successful.

```
<S:Envelope xmlns:S="http://schemas.xmlsoap.org/soap/envelope/">
  <S:Header>
    <work:WorkContext
      xmlns:work="http://oracle.com/weblogic/soap/workarea/">
      rO0ABXdOABd3ZWJsb2dpYy5hcHAub3JhY2xLWJhbQAAANYAAAA
        jd2VibG9naWMud29ya2FyZWEuU3RyaW5nV29ya0NvbnRleHQABjExLjEuMQAA
    </work:WorkContext>
  </S:Header>
  <S:Body>
    <ns2:InsertResponse xmlns:ns2="http://xmlns.oracle.com/bam"/>
  </S:Body>
</S:Envelope>
```

Summary

In this chapter, you learned how to populate Data Objects using the BAM Adapter, BPEL sensors, Enterprise Messaging Sources, and BAM Web services. You can also use the **Oracle Data Integrator** (**ODI**) and **Change Data Capture** (**CDC**) to load data into BAM. However, these topics are beyond the scope of this book, and you can refer to Oracle BAM documentation for more details.

In the next chapter, you will get some practical experience in building more complex reports using various templates, and learn advanced features in report design.

4
Designing BAM Reports

A BAM report/dashboard is a graphical user interface that can be used to display business activity information, analytics, and alerts. In the previous chapters, you have learned how to create Data Objects and move business data to them, which are the pre-requisites for building BAM reports that meet your needs. In this chapter, you will build a report, using various View types, to monitor order processing information and some KPIs in real time. You will start with a report that contains a single View, and then extend your report to include multiple Views. Finally, you will enable alerts, so that a notification e-mail will be sent if certain conditions are met.

As it is impractical to cover every report design topic in one chapter, we will focus on the key topics only, and you can use this chapter as a guideline for your future report design practices.

Designing a report that contains a single View

It is recommended to build a report using an incremental method, which is to start with a single View, and later extend it to include more View types.

Report design normally includes the following steps:

1. Specifying Data Objects and fields.
2. Performing data manipulation tasks.
3. Editing view properties.

In this section, you will learn how to build a single view report using a **List** View type, to track order processing information.

Specifying Data Objects and fields

Reports are rendered based on the contents of Data Objects. So, specifying Data Objects and their fields is the first step to create a report view. In this section, you will start to build a `BookstoreDemo` report using an incremental approach. The base View in the report is a list that is built with the **Updating Ordered List** view type, for displaying the contents of `/BookstoreDemo/Order` Data Object.

To create a view using the **Updating Ordered List** template, perform the following steps:

1. In **BAM Active Studio**, click on **Create A New Report** in the left pane. The layout page opens.

2. Click on **Single Tiled Report**.

3. Click on **Updating Ordered List** from the template.

4. An **Updating Ordered List** preview opens in the template, and the View editor opens at the bottom of the page. In the View editor, navigate to the `BookstoreDemo` folder, and select the **Order** Data Object.

5. Click on **Next**.

6. In the **Choose Data Fields** section, choose the following fields: `OrderID`, `CustomerID`, `OrderDate`, `OrderTotal`, and `OrderStatus`.

7. Click on **Next**.

8. Click on **Finish**. An **Updating Ordered List** view is displayed with the data as shown in the next screenshot.

9. Click on **Save Report**.

Updating Ordered List				
OrderID	CustomerID	OrderDate	OrderTotal	OrderStatusCode
1,001	108	9/27/2011 2:27:38 PM	50.97	Shipped
1,002	105	9/27/2011 10:10:38 AM	1,249.91	Processed
1,003	106	10/1/2011 2:27:38 PM	5,000	Shipped
1,004	104	7/22/2011 2:27:38 PM	879.93	Canceled
1,005	107	9/29/2011 2:27:39 PM	2,225.98	Shipped
1,006	102	10/1/2011 10:27:39 AM	551.86	Shipped
1,007	101	7/7/2011 2:27:39 PM	3,295.94	Shipped
1,008	103	9/30/2011 2:27:39 PM	100.97	Pending
1,009	109	9/30/2011 2:27:39 PM	12.99	Processed
1,010	102	9/25/2011 2:27:39 PM	1,259.98	Processed

The **Updating Ordered List** View type is one of the most commonly used List types. Unlike the **Streaming List**, which can only display Active Data as a result of the `Insert` operation in BAM Active Data Cache, or the `Updating List` operation for only showing updated records, the **Updating Ordered List** View supports displaying Active Data in an event of `Insert`, `Update`, `Upsert`, and `Delete` operations. If you would like to apply aggregate functions to data fields, use the **Collapsed List** View type.

Performing data manipulation tasks

In this section, you will perform the following data manipulation tasks:

- Adding filters
- Configuring surface prompts
- Adding calculated fields

Adding filters

Filters are search criteria that are used to restrict the query result. With filters enabled, a report View only shows the subset of data that meets your needs, instead of displaying all records by default. Applying appropriate filters is critical in report design, as it might significantly impact the usability and performance of your BAM reports/dashboards. For example, if you use a List/Table View to display a large volume of real-time data, it is a best practice to add filters to limit the number of records. Otherwise, the View will be hard to read, and the performance of the report will be impacted as well.

A filter expression is composed of one or more headers and entries. A **header** defines a logical operator, which is equivalent to a logical operator in Java, such as logical AND (`&&`) or logical OR (`||`). An **entry** defines a predicate that is evaluated to a Boolean value (`True` or `False`), on which a header performs logical operations. For example, a simple filter expression looks as follows:

This filter represents an `Entry1` or `Entry2` expression: `Entry1` is **OrderStatusCode is equal to New** and `Entry2` is **OrderStatusCode is equal to Pending**.

Creating a filter expression

To create a filter expression, perform the following steps:

1. Open the report that you have saved earlier. Click on **Edit** in the **Actions** pane to change the report to the edit mode.

2. Double-click the View that you want to add a filter expression, and then click on the **Filter** tab in the View editor.

3. Click on **add new header** in the **Filter** tab in the View editor window, and choose one of the following options:

    ○ **All**: A logical AND operator

    ○ **At least one**: A logical OR operator

    ○ **None**: A logical operator that is opposite to At least one

    ○ **Not all**: A logical operator that is opposite to All

4. Click on **add new entry** in the header, and specify predicates or criteria that follow this syntax:

   ```
   Field Comparison (Value, Field or Formula)
   ```

Suppose you want to filter orders whose status equals New; the filter entry or predicate should be OrderStatusCode is equal to New. Note that OrderStatusCode represents a Data Object field, is equal to is a comparison operator, and New is the value.

Now, let's create a filter in the **Updating Ordered List** View of the BookstoreDemo report. In this exercise, you will use the combination of headers and entries to build a complex filter expression that represents the following logic:

```
OrderDate == {CurrentDate} AND (OrderStatus == "New" OR OrderStatus
    == "Pending")
```

The completed filter expression should look as follows:

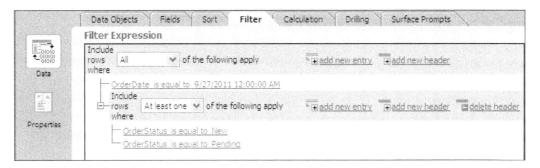

As you can see, these nested headers and entries are used to represent the
A AND (B OR C) logic.

Defining parameters

The filter entries that you saw earlier use hard-coded values for filter expressions.
In the real-world scenario, parameters are often used to dynamically pass values
to a filter expression.

Parameters are defined in the report-level. For different types of parameters and
requirements, the parameter definition has slight differences. The following are the
steps to define a parameter, which are used for the date/time comparison:

1. In the **Filter** tab, click on the entry that contains the hard-coded data/time.

2. Click on the **Options** button and then **New Parameter/Prompt**. The **Prompt
   and Parameter Creation** dialog-box appears.

3. In the **Name and Data Type** step, enter the following details:

   ° **Name**: Enter a name. For example, p_OrderDate.

   ° **Parameter Type**: This field is disabled and filled with a default type,
     which matches the Data Object field type in the entry.

   ° **Description**: This is an optional field.

   ° **Value**: Choose the **Prompt the user to specify a value** option.

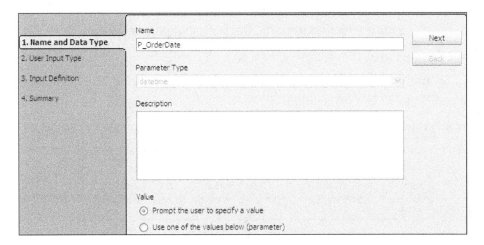

4. Click on **Next**.

5. In the **User Input Type** step, enter the following details:

   ○ **User input type**: Choose the **Type in** option to enter the value manually. The other option is **Choose from a list of field values**, which enables you to choose from the pre-defined list, derived from a Data Object.

   ○ **Prompt message text**: Enter a prompt text for this parameter.

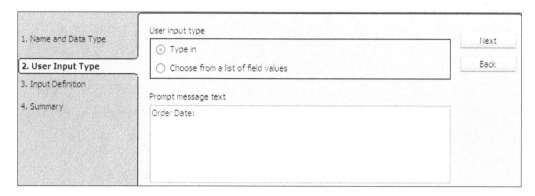

6. Click on **Next**.

7. In the **Input Definition** step, enter the following details:

   ○ **Default Value**: Select a default value for this parameter. For example, choose **System Datetime** for the p_OrderDate parameter.

   ○ **Value selection options**: Uncheck this property.

8. Click on **Next**.

9. Ensure that the **Compare Date only** checkbox is selected. Click on **OK** to finish the parameter configuration.

For the BookstoreDemo report, you need to create a filter expression as follows:

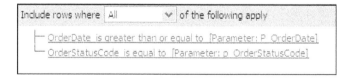

p_OrderDate is the parameter for the order creation date, and p_OrderStatusCode represents the order status code.

Now, if you open the report in BAM Active Viewer, it will prompt you to provide the parameter values before loading the report. For example, you can enter the following values when opening the report for the first time:

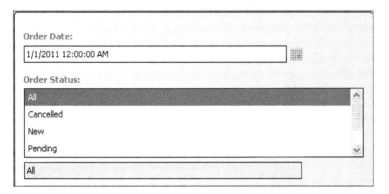

Configuring surface prompts

By default, parameters are defined in the report level. Therefore, they are not visible in the **View title** or **View area** after a report is reloaded. To change this behavior, you can configure surface prompts to display prompts in the **View title** or **View area**.

In the BookstoreDemo report, configure the P_OrderDate and the P_OrderStatusCode parameters to be displayed in **View title**.

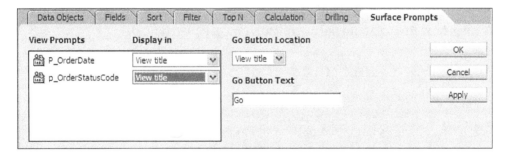

Adding calculated fields

When designing a View, sometimes you will need to include calculated fields that are not listed in the Data Objects. A **calculated field** is a field that is the result of a calculation, using one or more existing fields.

> You can create calculated fields in either a report scope or a Data Object scope. Calculated fields in a report scope are exclusive to a particular report, thus they cannot be reused by other reports. So, it is a design decision whether calculated fields reside in the report scope or the Data Object scope. Regardless of the scope the calculated fields belong to, the calculation will be used to construct SQL queries as a part of the SELECT clause.

To create a calculated field in a report scope, click on the **Calculation** tab in the **View** editor, build an expression using the expression builder, and click on *Enter*.

Suppose you need to create a new calculated field called PriorityHandling to implement the following logic: If {OrderTotal} >= 2000, then the PriorityHandling flag will be set to Yes. Otherwise, leave this field blank.

The calculation should look as follows:

```
If ({OrderTotal} >= 2000)
Then ("YES")
```

You can also enhance the calculation by adding HTML codes. The following example illustrates how to add an image as content for a calculated field:

```
If ({OrderTotal} >= 2000)
   Then (Concat(Concat("<img src='../Images/round_green16px.gif'
     alt='","Yes"),"' />"))
Else ("")
```

This HTML code uses a relative path of the Report Server's current directory to reference round_green16px.gif, which is an image shipped with Oracle BAM product. The current directory for Report Server is <BAM domain dir>/ servers/<bam_server1>/tmp/_WL_user/oracle-bam_11.1.1/eow41x/ war/13846/reportserver.

By default, the content in a calculated field is formatted as a `String` type. So, to render the HTML code for the `PriorityHandling` field, you need to perform the following steps:

1. Click on **Properties** in the View editor.
2. Click on the **Value Format** tab.
3. Select the `PriorityHandling` field from the **Apply To** list, and choose **HTML** from the **Category** list.
4. Click on **Apply** or **OK** to save the change.

If the calculated field is configured correctly, you will see the following list view with HTML contents:

Order Tracking	Order Date: 2011-01-01T00:0	Order Status: All		Go

CustomerID	OrderDate	OrderID	OrderStatusCode	OrderTotal	PriorityHandling
108	9/27/2011 2:27:	1,001	Shipped	50.97	
105	9/27/2011 10:10	1,002	Processed	1,249.91	
106	10/1/2011 2:27:	1,003	Shipped	5,000	●
104	7/22/2011 2:27:	1,004	Canceled	879.98	
107	9/29/2011 2:27:	1,005	Shipped	2,225.98	●
102	10/1/2011 10:27	1,006	Shipped	551.86	
101	7/7/2011 2:27:39	1,007	Shipped	3,295.94	●
103	9/30/2011 2:27:	1,008	Pending	100.97	
109	9/30/2011 2:27:	1,009	Processed	12.99	

It is recommended to create a calculated field in the Data Object, provided you want to share the calculated field in various views or reports. If calculated fields are specific to a report, create them in the report scope. From a performance perspective, it makes no difference by switching from Data Object scope to report scope for calculated fields. However, the calculated field expression builder has syntax verification in the Active Studio and not in Architect. Use copy-paste into the Active Studio calculation expression builder to verify the syntax, if required.

Editing View properties

Another task for designing a report View is to define its properties (such as the report tile, text font, format, and alignment), Active Data rendering behavior, and so on.

In this section, you will format the value of the `OrderTotal` field as a currency. Perform the following steps to change this view property:

1. Open the report that you have saved earlier. Click on **Edit** in the **Actions** pane to change the report to the edit mode.

2. Double-click the **Updating Ordered List** View.

3. In the View editor, click on the **Properties** icon and the **Value Format** tab.

4. Change the format as shown in the following screenshot:

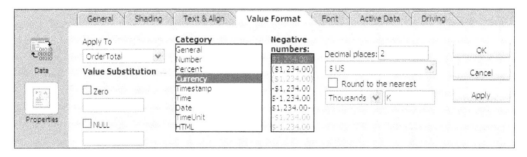

5. Click on **OK**. The `OrderTotal` column should show values in currency format.

6. Click on **Save**.

View properties settings vary from one report to another, which is determined by the design requirements and specifications. If you are interested in finding more specific information, it is available in the *User's Guide for Oracle Business Activity Monitoring* in the *Fusion Middleware documentation library*.

Extending your report to include multiple Views

In the previous section, you learned how to create a `BookstoreDemo` report that contains a single View. In this section, you will learn how to extend your report to include multiple Views. The following View types will be used to extend the report:

- Driving from a master View to a detail View
- Adding a Gauge View
- Adding a Chart View

Driving from a master view to a detail view

Sometimes, you will need to create a master View and a detail View, so that you can drive the content from the master View to the detail View. To make the driving work, you need to extend your report as follows:

- Create a detail View to display the order items.
- Enable driving in the master View. In this example, the **Updating Ordered List** you just created will serve as the master View. Clicking on a particular record in the master View will drive the detail View to reflect the changes.

Creating a detail View

You need to create a detail View using the **Updating Ordered List** View type. Here are the key steps to create this View:

1. In **BAM Active Studio**, click on the **Shared Report** tab, then click on the report that you created before.
2. Click on **Edit** in the **Actions** pane. The report becomes editable.

3. Select and resize the single View, then click on the **Insert View** icon in the toolbar. A View template appears, as shown in the following screenshot:

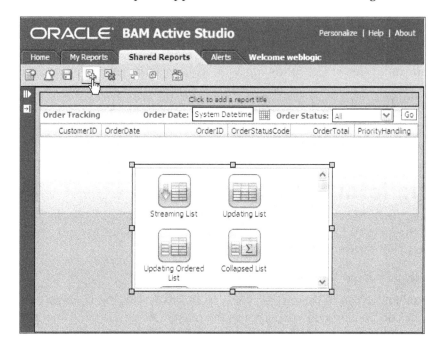

4. Click on **Updating Ordered List**.

5. Select the `Order_Item` Data Object in the `BookstoreDemo` folder and all its fields.

6. Create a filter as shown in the following screenshot. `P_OrderID` is a parameter that represents an `OrderID` prompt.

7. In the **Surface Prompts** tab, configure `P_OrderID` to be displayed in View title.

8. Click on **OK** to finish editing.

9. Click on **Save Report As**, and enter `OrderTrackingReport_Multiview`.

Enabling driving

Driving is enabled by mapping the field values in the master View to the corresponding parameters. When driving happens, the matching parameters are populated with field values from the master report. If one of these parameters is defined as a prompt in the detail report, then the detail View will reload based on the new parameter value populated by the master View.

 Not all View types support driving. Driving is only available in the **List** and **Crosstab** Views.

To enable driving from the master View to the detail view, you need to perform the following steps:

1. In the report edit mode, double-click the master View.
2. Click on **Properties** and the **Driving** tab.
3. In **Map Fields to Prompts/Parameters**, choose P_OrderID, and map it to the OrderID field.

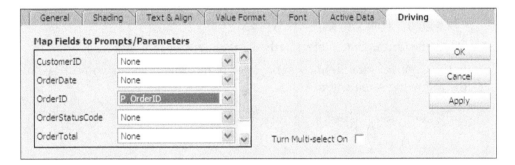

4. Click on **OK** to finish the configuration.
5. Click on **Save Report**. Now, you should have a master View and a detail View. Click on one row in the master View, and the detail view should change accordingly.

Apart from driving, you can also use the **drilling** function to add interactions between different views. Drilling allows users to drill through the same View based on hierarchies, or drill across a different view by passing parameters. When driving is enabled, both participating views are visible. However, when drilling across is configured, only one view (either the original view or the destination view) is displayed, as one view replaces another when rendering.

To enable driving, the detail report must have prompts/parameters defined in the filter. For the master report, you can only define driving or drilling, but not both. If drilling is enabled, it will override the driving configuration.

Adding a Gauge View

In this section, you will learn to expand your report to include two Gauge views, for displaying how long an order has been processed internally, and how long an order has been awaiting shipment on an average.

The following are the key steps to add a Gauge view for displaying the order processing time:

1. Open the same report that you saved before, and then click on **Edit** in the **Actions** pane to open it in an edit mode.

2. Resize the existing views, and rearrange the layout. Go to the end of this section to view the layout of this report. Click on the **Insert View** icon in the toolbar.

3. Click on the **Dial Gauge** View type.

4. Select the **Order** Data Object in the BookstoreDemo folder.

5. In the **Choose Data Fields** section, specify the data fields as you can see in the following screenshot:

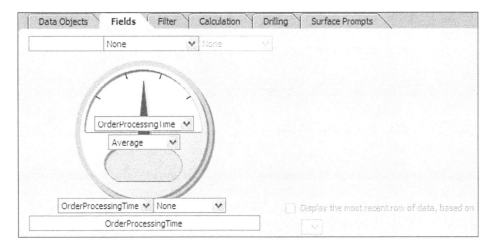

6. Add the following filter. I assume that you are already familiar with the methods for creating filters. To view the detailed steps, refer to the *Adding filters* section that you saw before.

7. Click on **Properties** and the **General** tab, and set the title to `Order Processing Time`.

8. Click on **OK** to finish editing.

9. Repeat the previous steps (from *step 1* to *step 8*) to create another Gauge view, for displaying how long an order has been awaiting shipment.

Use the view to display the `OrderShippingTime` field.

10. Save the report. Now, the report should look similar to the one in the following screenshot. Click on one row in the master View (the first **Updating Ordered List** View that you created). The processing time and shipment time should be seen in this Gauge view.

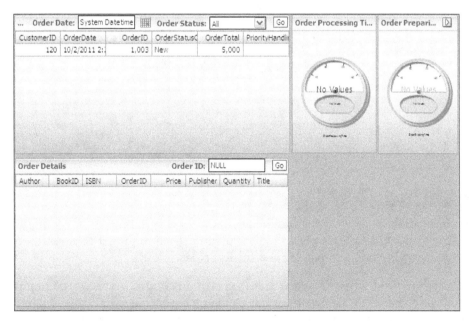

A **Gauge view** is a KPI View that is used to display a single value in the view area. If no aggregation is specified, the backend Data Object should only contain one row of data. Otherwise, it will throw an exception.

Adding a Chart View

Now, continue to extend your report to include a Chart view, to display the number of orders grouped by order status. The specific steps for doing this have already been covered in *Chapter 2, Designing Your First Data Objects and Reports*. The key configuration for this View type is to specify the group by field (OrderStatus), function (Count), and the View value (OrderID), while the rest of steps are very similar to the other View types.

After including this Chart view, the report should look as follows:

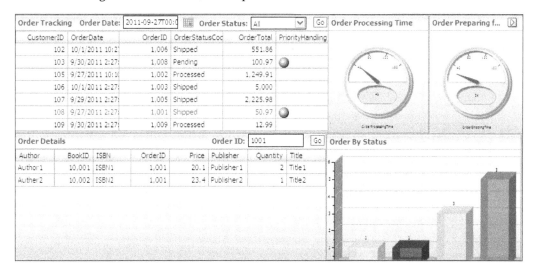

Enabling BAM alerts

BAM alerts are a set of rules that define events and actions. If alerts are configured, the BAM server will continuously monitor the information for certain conditions, and execute the related actions defined in alert rules.

Alert rules are fired when an event occurs or certain conditions are met. Examples of events are: in a specific amount of time, when a report changes, when a data field changes in a data object, or when a data field changes to meet specified conditions, and so on.

Actions define a set of operations that the BAM server can perform, for example, sending e-mails, invoking web services or Java code, and so on. In a typical production environment, alerts are also used for purging data from the Data Objects, which can be scheduled for older data at non-peak hours.

Alert actions can be conditional or unconditional. A **conditional action** means there is an IF condition associated with an action. Only if the condition is met will an action be executed. An **unconditional action** is an action that always gets executed when an event occurs.

In this section, you will create an alert that defines the following rule: *If the processing time for a particular order exceeds 120 hours, then a notification e-mail will be sent to the system administrator.*

Creating a BAM alert

You can create an alert in either the BAM Architect or BAM Active Studio web application. In this section, you will learn how to use the BAM Active Studio to set up an alert. Using the BAM Architect will not be covered here, as the web dialog-box for setting up alerts are the same. To create an alert rule in BAM Active Studio, perform the following steps:

1. In BAM Active Studio, click on the **Alerts** tab and then **Create A New Alert**. The **Rule Creation And Edit** web page dialog-box opens.

2. Click on **Create A Rule**.

3. Enter a rule name for this alert.

4. In the **Select an Event** section, choose **When a data field in a data object meets specified conditions**. The When this data field has a condition of x, then run as weblogic expression appears in the **Rule Expression** section.

5. Click on this data field that has a condition of the x expression link. A **Field Selection** dialog-box appears.

6. Choose the /BookstoreDemo/Order Data Object, and create a new filter: OrderProcessingTime is greater than or equal to 120 (Hours). Click on **OK** to close the **Field Selection** dialog.

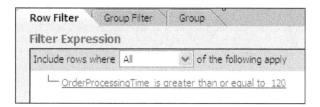

7. Click on **Next**. In the **Select an Action** section, choose **Send a message via email**. A new rule - **Send create message via email to select user** - appears in the **Rule Expression** section.

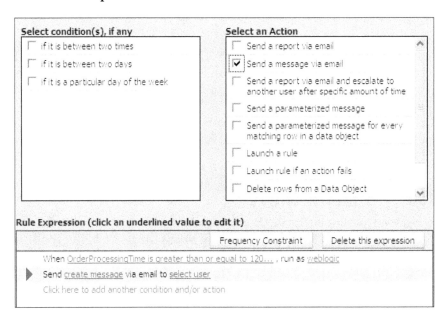

8. Click on the **create message** link. The **Alert Message** dialog-box appears.

9. Edit the subject and body of the message. You can add dynamic contents by inserting Data Object fields into the e-mail subject or body, as shown in the following screenshot:

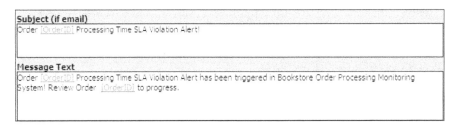

10. Click on the **select user** to add the receipt e-mail address.

11. In the **select users** dialog-box, you can choose a user from the list.

12. Click on **OK** to finish the configuration. A new rule appears in the **Alert Rules** table.

> When a user is selected as an e-mail recipient in an e-mail action, the user's e-mail ID is automatically retrieved from the identity store (LDAP server), integrated with Oracle WebLogic Server. If you want to specify another e-mail as the recipient address, then specify the e-mail ID in the **select users** dialog-box, and set the AlertActionAllowExternalEmail attribute to true in the following file. Note that it requires BAM server restart.
>
> ```
> <BAMDomain>/config/fmwconfig/servers/<bam_
>     server1>/applications/oracle-bam_11.1.1/config/
>     BAMCommonConfig.xml
> ```

Configuring User Messaging Service

User Messaging Service (UMS) provides a single consolidated bi-directional user messaging service, which can be integrated with other Fusion Middleware components. UMS supports a variety of messaging channels, such as e-mail, IM (XMPP), SMS (SMPP), and voice.

BAM utilizes the e-mail service provided by UMS. To configure UMS, perform the following steps:

1. Log in to Oracle Enterprise Manager (EM) Fusion Middleware control. The EM URL is http://hostname:port/em.

2. Expand **User Messaging Service** in the farm tree.

3. Right-click on `usermessagingdriver-email(bam_server1)`, and click on **Email Driver Properties**. The **Email Driver Properties** page appears.

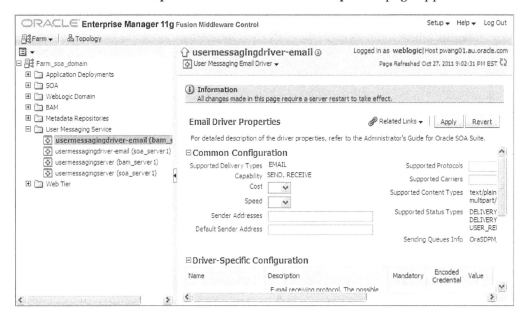

4. In the **Driver-Specific Configuration** section, set the following properties:
   - **OutgoingMailServer**: Enter the e-mail server hostname.
   - **OutgoingMailServerPort**: Enter the e-mail server port number. The default port is 25.
   - **OutgoingDefaultFromAddr**: Enter the sender's default e-mail address as the **From address of the e-mail**.
   - **Debug**: This is optional. Checking this property will print the debug information in the log file.

5. Click on **Apply**.

6. Restart the BAM server to make the changes take effect.

Summary

In this chapter, you gained some experience of building a report by using an incremental approach. Through these report design practices, you learned how to use advanced report features, such as filters, calculated fields, driving from one view to another, and alerts.

In the next chapter, you will learn about some more advanced topics, such as performing load testing and tuning.

5
Testing BAM Applications

Testing is a very important phase in the software development lifecycle for BAM applications. Testing BAM applications carries unique challenges, and requires a specialized approach. However, the testing function for this highly dynamic technology area is at a very early stage of maturity.

In this chapter, you will learn the following topics:

- Introducing BAM testing methodologies
- Testing BAM Data Objects
- Testing BAM report views
- Performing end-to-end testing

Introducing BAM testing methodologies

In this section, you will learn the challenges for testing BAM applications, and the testing methodologies for BAM.

First of all, let's take a look at the challenges for testing BAM applications:

- **Lack of knowledge**: Testing BAM applications requires testers to gain a thorough understanding of BAM key concepts, such as Data Object/report design principles, the technologies used for populating Data Objects, Active Data processing, and so on.

- **Lack of tools**: There are no testing tools in the market that offer features for automated testing or functional testing for BAM applications.

- **Lack of standard methodologies**: While standard methodologies exist for software testing, there seems to be no industry-wide view on the suggested approaches and methodologies for testing BAM.

An ideal methodology for testing BAM applications should include a test strategy, a test plan, and test cases that provide adequate coverage in various phases of data processing. For example, when testing a BAM application, you should develop test cases that can be used to verify data processing in different components, such as Active Data Cache, Report Server, and the Web browser.

Developing a test strategy

The testing strategy for testing BAM applications should include the following key elements:

- **Testing procedures**: The levels of testing, such as unit, integration, and **User Acceptance Testing** (**UAT**) should be documented
- **Types of testing**: All the various types of testing, such as compatibility and regression, should be mentioned

Developing a test plan

For every level and type of testing, you should have a comprehensive test plan, including the following key points:

- **Scope of testing**: The scope of testing refers to the functional and/or non-functional requirements, such as Data Object testing, performance testing, and so on.
- **Testing techniques and tools**: The testing techniques can be White-Box testing or Black-Box testing.
- **Tools**: Software testing tools can be used to facilitate testing practices.
- **Test Data Preparation**: The test data can either be the duplication of a subset of production data (ensures that customer's confidential data is not used for such purposes), or a set of data generated from scratch. When using the self-generated data, ensure you understand the range of possible values for various fields.

Developing test cases

Unlike other applications, where testing is focused on user interfaces, BAM applications are data-orientated (Active Data), and thus carry unique requirements for developing test cases.

The major objective of executing test cases is to verify data consistency and accuracy, especially in the event of Active Data scenarios. And in general, these test cases should cover the following areas:

- Testing BAM Data Objects
- Testing BAM report views
- Performing end-to-end testing

    ◦ Testing Active Data processing
    ◦ Performing **load testing**

In the following sections, you will learn the testing requirements and guidelines for testing BAM applications.

Testing BAM Data Objects

In BAM applications, everything revolves around data and Active Data processing. Business users may rely on the Active Data movement in real time to make decisions. Therefore, timeliness and accuracy of data becomes very critical for the usability of the system.

From a quality assurance perspective, the key objective of testing Data Objects is to ensure a high level of data quality, such as data accuracy and consistency. Examples of data quality issues include:

- Duplicate data or incomplete data extracted from data source
- Data losses
- Incorrect calculations or aggregations
- Incorrect lookup values through Data Object lookup methods

Preparing test data

Business data can be moved from various data sources (BPEL processes, SOA composites, JMS destinations, and Web services, and so on) to Oracle BAM. As different data sources can have different requirements for data formats, you need to prepare the test data for each data source from which the business data are extracted.

The message flow in the `Bookstore` demo application is shown in the following diagram:

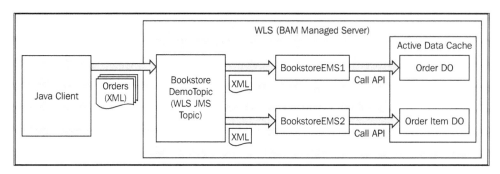

A Java client sends XML documents to the `BookstoreDemoTopic` WebLogic server JMS topic. A sample XML payload looks as follows:

```
<Order xmlns="http://www.packtpub.com/5443/BookstoreDemo">
  <OrderID>100000</OrderID>
  <CustomerID>101</CustomerID>
  <OrderStatusCode>Shipped</OrderStatusCode>
  <OrderTotal>20.1</OrderTotal>
  <OrderDate>2011-10-06T10:09:45.0000000+08:00</OrderDate>
  <OrderReceivedDate>
    2011-10-06T10:09:45.0000000+08:00
  </OrderReceivedDate>
  <OrderProcessedDate>
    2011-10-06T14:09:45.0000000+08:00
  </OrderProcessedDate>
  <OrderShippedDate>
    2011-10-08T10:09:45.0000000+08:00
   </OrderShippedDate>
  <OrderItems>
    <Item>
      <OrderID>100000</OrderID>
      <BookID>10001</BookID>
      <Title>Title1</Title>
      <Publisher>Publisher1</Publisher>
      <ISBN>ISBN1</ISBN>
      <Author>Author1</Author>
      <Price>20.1</Price>
      <Quantity>1</Quantity>
    </Item>
  </OrderItems>
</Order>
```

Two EMSs (`BookstoreEMS1` and `BookstoreEMS2`) are configured to consume messages from the JMS topic and populate the `Order` and `Order_Item` Data Objects, respectively.

In the `Bookstore` demo application, the Java client includes the following classes:

- `MyJMSMessageProducer.java`: This is the Java class that is used to connect to JMS server and publish messages

- `XMLPayloadGenerator.java`: This is the Java class that is used to generate the test data

- `MyLoadGenerator.java`: This is the Java class that is used to simulate the load for load-testing purposes

These Java classes just provide a guideline for writing your own clients to test EMS and BAM data feed. If the BAM Adapter or Web services APIs are used to populate BAM Data Objects, you can use BPEL processes, or a Web services testing tool, such as `SOAPUI`, to generate the load.

Testing data mappings and transformations

Data mappings and transformations are configured through EMS. The major objective of this testing is to ensure the validity and correctness of data mappings and transformations when business data are moving to BAM though EMS.

In this section, you will learn the testing methods and guidelines for verifying data mappings and transformations for EMS. Note the testing methods may vary if a different integration solution (for example, the BAM Adapter or ODI) is used.

Testing XML to Data Object mappings

The purpose of this testing is to verify the functionality of XML to Data Object mappings. In many cases, business field definitions in upstream data sources are different than BAM Data Object field definitions. So you should always keep the data accuracy and validation in mind, when testing XML to Data Object mapping.

Consider the following rules when preparing test data:

- **Data constraints**: Follow the data constraints in the upstream data source. For example, the `unique` constraint, and the `Nullable` constraint
- **Data field format**: The `data` field format should comply with the upstream data source format definition
- **Data precision**: Use the data precision defined in the upstream data source

To verify the test result, you can either review the newly-updated records in the BAM Architect web application, or you can build an SQL query to query the BAM Data Object underlying database table (called `dataset` in BAM). Using the SQL approach is more realistic, especially when the Data Object contains thousands of records.

You can find a Data Object's dataset name in the BAM Architect Web application. As shown in the following screenshot, `_Order1` is the dataset name for the `Order` **Data Object**:

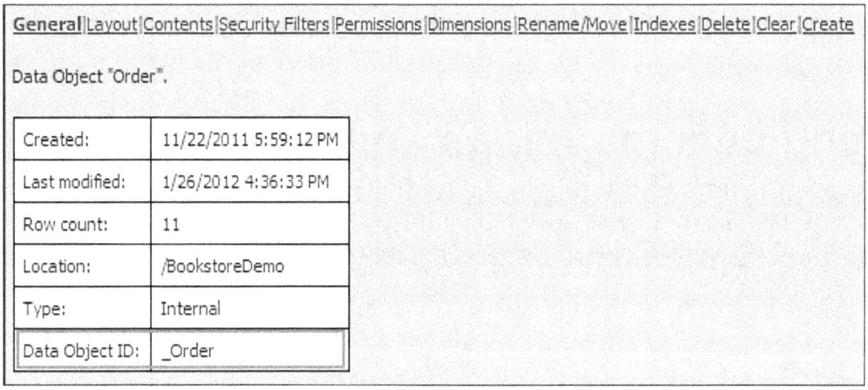

Testing XML transformations

EMS utilizes an XSL transformation code to pre-process an original XML payload received from a JMS topic/queue, so that the transformation result can be used for direct XML to Data Object field-mapping.

There are many tools available to test XSL code. In this section, you will learn how to use the Oracle `JDeveloper` to test XSL transformations.

To use `JDeveloper` to validate an XSL code, perform the following steps:

1. Open `JDeveloper`, and click **File | New...** from the menu. The **New Gallery** window appears.

2. Select **Applications** in the **Categories** pane, and **Generic Application** in the **Items** pane. Click on **OK**.

3. In the **Create Generic Application – Step 1 of 2** window, enter an application name and a directory. Click on **Next**.

4. In the **Create Generic Application – Step 2 of 2** window, enter a project name, leave other fields unchanged, and click on **Finish**. The new application and project name appears in the **Application Navigator**.

5. Right-click on the project name in the **Application Navigator** pane, and click on **New...** to open a **New Gallery** window.

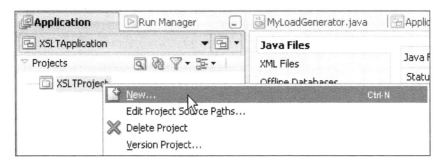

6. In the **New Gallery** window, select XML in the **Categories** pane, and **XSL Style Sheet** in the **Items** pane. Click on **OK**.

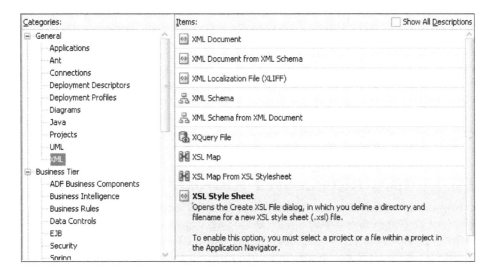

7. Enter a name for the **XSL transformation code**, and click on **OK**. A new XSL file opens in the editor.

8. Copy **XSL codes** into the file.

9. Click on **File | Save All**.

10. To test the XSL transformation code, right-click on the XSL file in the **Application Navigator**, and click on **Run**.

11. In the **XSLT Settings** window, specify the input **XML File** and **Output File**. Click on **OK**.

12. Inspect the output file to verify the result.

You may consider using a testing framework or a tool to automate the validation of data conversion (mappings and transformations). For example, you can first create a test step in SOAPUI, a testing tool to send XML data to EMS, and then create a JDBC test step to verify the content in the BAM repository database.

Testing calculated and lookup fields

Validating calculated fields and lookup fields are two critical tasks in testing Data Objects. Unlike Data Object fields, whose data accuracy and validity are primarily determined by upstream data sources, the data quality of calculated fields and lookup fields are determined by expressions defined in the Data Object level.

Testing calculated fields

A **calculated field** is a field whose value is derived from other Data Object fields. Calculation expression sometimes produces unexpected or invalid results. For example, the expression Sum (Field A) /Sum (Field B) may potentially cause a typical divided by zero error, and the expression Field A/Field B may produce unexpected data precision issues (for example, the calculation of 4/3 is 1, instead of 1.3333).

So, it is a best practice to build test cases that cover all realistic boundary value conditions, based on the existing formulas for calculated fields.

In the Bookstore Demo application, we use the following formula to calculate the order processing time:

```
if ((OrderProcessedDate == NULL) || (OrderReceivedDate == NULL))
   then (0)
else ((OrderProcessedDate - OrderReceivedDate)/3600)
```

To fully test thid formula, you need to create test cases to cover the following scenarios:

- OrderProcessedDate == Null or OrderReceivedDate == Null
- OrderProcessedDate and OrderReceivedDate both contain valid values

 To test calculated fields, you don't have to use a Java client that sends the test data to BAM through EMS. Instead, you can simply use the BAM Architect web application to modify specific data fields, which are a part of the calculation.

Testing lookup fields

As you saw in *Chapter 2, Designing your First Data Objects and Reports*, BAM internally uses the LEFT OUTER JOIN to determine the values of lookup fields. So, from the quality-assurance perspective, the best way to verify the lookup result is to run the SQL queries on BAM datasets.

In the Bookstore Demo application, the Order Data Object has a field called CustomerMembership, whose definition is as follows:

```
Lookup Data Object:
/BookstoreDemo/Customer
Lookup Field(s):
Membership
Matching fields:
CustomerID = CustomerID
```

According to this definition, the value of `CustomerMembership` is derived from the lookup field `Membership` in the `/BookstoreDemo/Customer` Data Object, if the condition `Order.CustomerID = Customer.CustomerID` is met.

In this case, you can use an SQL query to test lookup fields. The following steps are the guidelines to build and run test cases:

1. Write a Java program to load a sample data into this Data Object.
2. Write an SQL query that combines values from this Data Object and the lookup Data Object. For example, the SQL query can be as follows:

```
SELECT DISTINCT "_Order1"."_CustomerID", "_Customer"."_Membership"
FROM "_Order1" LEFT OUTER JOIN "_Customer"
ON "_Order1"."_CustomerID" = "_Customer"."_CustomerID"
```

3. Inspect the SQL query result to determine if there are any mismatches for the fields.

 You may look at the content page of the Data Object in the BAM Architect Web application, to determine the outcome of the lookup result. However, the SQL approach is more appropriate, if automated testing is to be performed.

Testing BAM report Views

A **BAM dashboard** or **report** may contain multiple views, and each view in a report is comprised of view data and view properties. This section provides guidelines for testing BAM report views, which can help you to build test cases to verify the functionalities of a BAM report.

Testing View data

View data is the key component for designing BAM report views. To perform comprehensive testing on view data for a particular view, you have to build test cases to cover the following functional areas:

- Data Object and field selections - verify if the field selections and their display orders meet application requirements.
- Verify if report filter conditions are set properly as per the requirements.
- Verify if drilling/driving are configured properly as per the requirements, and if they work as expected.

- Calculations - report-level calculations are similar to Data Object calculated fields. You need to build test cases to verify the validity and accuracy of the calculation result.
- Verify if Sort and TopN work as expected.
- Verify that the Views using time or timestamps show the correct time/time-zone information.

 It would be easier to verify the test result using a small set of data, rather than a large amount of data. Ensure that no other users use the system or trigger data mutations in any other way while testing functional parts of a report, as described in the following sections.

Testing View properties

The major objective of testing View properties is to verify if the display characteristics of a report View type meet the application specifications and requirements.

The following checklist gives you some guidelines for testing View properties:

- Verify if report layouts are set properly as per the requirement
- Verify if the fonts, the colors, and the styles are set properly and consistently as per the requirement
- Verify if value formats comply with the requirements
- If a report uses multiple tabs, check whether the tab name is meaningful and contains correct sub views

Performing end-to-end testing

It is very important to start testing Data Objects and reports earlier in the development life cycle for your BAM applications. Once the data quality and report functionality have been verified, it is the time to conduct end-to-end testing to verify the message flow and performance.

End-to-end testing is an application-level testing that verifies the system components integration and the complete flow of data under normal or load conditions. When performing the end-to-end testing for BAM applications, you should focus on the following areas:

- Verification of data flow (Active Data processing)
- Verification of performance under load conditions

Testing Active Data processing

Oracle BAM leverages the push-based mechanism to deliver continuous data changes to frontend web browsers in real time. So, testing the whole message flow to ensure the Active Data processing functionality is critical for the quality assurance purpose.

The following diagram depicts the message flow in the `Bookstore Demo` application:

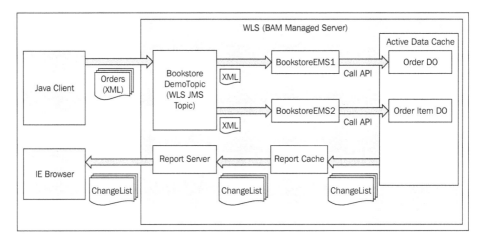

An example of this end-to-end message flow looks as follows:

1. An external client publishes XML messages to the `BookstoreDemoTopic` JMS Topic.

2. Two EMSs (`BookstoreEMS1` and `BookstoreEMS2`) consume these XML messages from the topic, then transform and send the data to the `Order` and `Order_Item` Data Objects, respectively.

3. If certain conditions are met, a set of `ChangeLists` are produced in the BAM Active Data Cache.

4. `ChangeLists` are then pushed through Report Cache and Report Server to IE browsers, which accordingly update report views.

You can use the black-box testing method to verify this functionality, so that no specific knowledge of the application's code/internal structure is required. Test cases are built around specifications and requirements, and should include the following elements:

- Data input to produce Active Data
- Expected results

In the `Bookstore Demo` application, which is the XML payload produced by the Java client, you should expect to observe the real-time data changes displayed in one or more report views in the IE browser.

Active Data for a particular report are generated by active `ViewSets` in the BAM Active Data Cache. So, to ensure that Active Data are produced as expected, you must have the specific report opened at the client side throughout the testing period.

Performing load testing

Load testing is the process of measuring a system's behavior under normal and heavy load conditions. The testing result can help to identify the maximum operating capacity of your current system as well as potential performance bottlenecks.

Load testing for BAM has its own characteristics as BAM applications are more data-driven than user interaction-driven. When performing load testing for BAM, the major objective is to evaluate the accuracy and performance of the end-to-end Active Data processing.

In this section, we will look at the following key elements for load testing:

- Generating a load
- Monitoring performance
- Analyzing results

Generating a load

You can generate a load on the current system by duplicating production or UAT data streams, or you can simply simulate production message rates by writing your code in languages that you are familiar with.

Due to the lack of load testing tools suitable for BAM, we will write our own Java client to generate the load, and rely on the performance matrix in the Enterprise Manager to measure the performance.

In the `Bookstore Demo` application, we use a `while` loop in a custom Java code to simulate the load (the rate of data movement from a JMS topic to BAM). The logic within the `while` loop is very simple.

Firstly, it calls the `generateXML` method of the `XMLPayloadGenerator` class to generate an XML payload.

```
String xmlPayload = xmlPayloadGenerator.generateXML(orderID,
    customerID,bookID, random.nextInt(4),random.nextDouble() * 1000);
```

Secondly, it invokes the `publish` method of the `MyJMSMessageProducer` class to publish the payload to a configurable JMS topic.

```
myJMSMessageProducer.publish(xmlPayload);
```

Finally, it invokes the `Thread.sleep` method to suspend the current thread for a specified time.

```
Thread.sleep(currStoptime);
```

When you run this Java program, it will generate a load by publishing XML messages to a JMS topic. For different technologies that you use to move business data to BAM, you might need different types of load generators. For example, if business data are moved from an SOA composite to a BAM server through a BAM Adapter, you may consider a Web service testing tool, such as `LoadUI`, to generate a load for the SOA composite.

Monitoring performance

Monitoring the performance of BAM applications requires monitoring BAM server performance, as well as overall system performance, such as **Java Virtual Machine** (JVM) that runs a BAM server, the server side CPU and memory utilizations, the client side CPU and memory utilizations, and so on. In this section, we will focus on the usage of the BAM server-specific performance monitoring tool.

Oracle Enterprise Manager 11g Fusion Middleware Control provides a monitoring tool to monitor key performance metrics of BAM servers, which help to determine performance bottlenecks. To use the monitoring tool, perform the following steps:

1. Log in to **Enterprise Manager 11g Fusion Middleware Control**. The URL is `http://hostname:port/em`.

2. Expand **BAM** in the **Farm** pane, and click on `OracleBamWeb`.

3. In the `OracleBamWeb` section, select **BAM Web | Monitoring | Performance Summary**. The **Performance Summary** page opens.

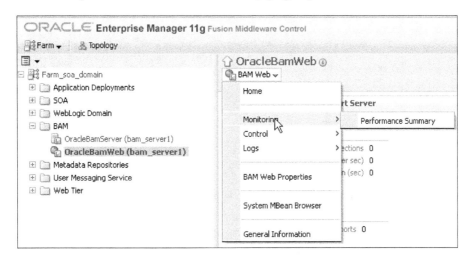

4. In the **Performance Summary** page, click on the **Show Metric Palette** button.

5. Select the following metrics:

   ° **Open Connections**: This metric collects the number of open HTTP connections through which Active Data are pushed from a BAM server to its clients

   ° **Open Reports**: This metric collects the number of reports, which are opened by the clients

   ° **Open Viewsets**: This metric collects the number of **ViewSets**, which are opened in a BAM server

   ° **Activity Message Rates (per sec)**: This metric collects the activity message (Active Data) rates, per second

   ° **Average Time To Open Viewsets (in sec)**: This metric collects the average time to open **ViewSets** in a Report Server

The following screenshot shows the performance summary for a BAM Report Server. You can click on the **Table View** to view the actual data for the charts.

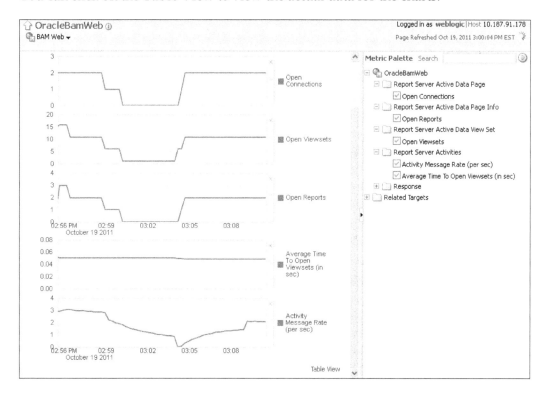

Analyzing results

In many cases, analyzing performance issues can be very challenging and time-consuming, as systems are getting more and more complex today, and the root causes of these issues vary from one system to another.

The recommended starting point for analyzing BAM performance issues is to review the performance summary report that you saw earlier. In this section, we will provide some guidelines and case studies which can help you to gain some experience on how to identify potential performance bottlenecks using these charts.

Identifying closed connections

The **Open Connections** chart refers to the number of persistent HTTP connections through which a BAM Report server sends `ChangeLists`, asynchronously, to IE browsers.

A BAM Report server only maintains one HTTP connection per client machine (based on its IP address), for pushing ChangeLists to IE browsers on this client. Any subsequent HTTP requests sent by the same client machine will receive Changelists through the same HTTP connection maintained in the Report server. These connections are only closed when no further reports are opened in the client machine.

So, by looking at this chart, you can determine if there are any closed connection issues between a client machine and a BAM server.

Identifying performance bottlenecks for report loading

ViewSets are opened in a BAM server when reports are loaded in web browsers for the first time. So, you can use the **Average Time To Open Viewsets (in sec)** chart to determine performance bottlenecks for report loading.

Let's take a look at an example. Assume that you encounter a performance issue, which is one particular report takes a long time (4 minutes) to open for the first time. Let's see how you can use this chart to analyze this problem.

First of all, you need to find the time frame when the issue was first detected. Then, you find the chart value at this time frame. If the figure is high, say 120 seconds, the ViewSet opening may be the key contributor for the overall performance degradation. In this case, you will need to further investigate the possible causes, such as underlying BAM repository performance, SQL query performance, JVM memory settings, and so on.

If the figure is low, say only 0.6 seconds, then it means that the report server processing should not cause the performance issues. Therefore, instead of looking into the BAM server-side problems, you need to focus on analyzing potential networking or client-side issues.

Identifying Active Data processing issues

The **Activity Message Rates (per sec)** metric can be used to analyze the Active Data processing issues.

Let's take a look at an example. Assume that the problem is that a BAM report stops refreshing Active Data in a browser. Let's see how you can use the **Activity Message Rates (per sec)** metric to analyze this issue.

If the activity message rates are high, then it is very likely that the report server has successfully processed Active Data. In this case, you should look at the IE browser to figure out whether it has successfully received or processed `ChangeLists` (Active Data payload).

If the figures are low, then you can rule out the client-side problem, as the metric indicates the `ChangeLists` may not arrive in the report server in the first place. In this case, you should analyze other BAM server-side components, such as Active Data Cache and Report Cache, to further break down the problems.

Summary

In this chapter, you learned BAM testing methodologies, the testing requirements, and guidelines for testing BAM Data Objects, report views, and Active Data processing under normal and load conditions.

Due to the lack of knowledge, tools, and standard methodologies that test the BAM applications carry unique challenges and require specialized approaches. You should keep in mind that ensuring data accuracy and consistency for Active Data processing always is the key objective of different level or types of testing.

6
Managing BAM Securities

BAM securities requirements vary from one system to another. Nevertheless, the basic things remain the same. For a BAM application, you have to ensure your resources, such as Data Objects, reports, and the BAM web applications, are securely protected, so that only authenticated and authorized users can access the information. Apart from these, you also need to consider the security issues during the data transmission between clients and servers. Keeping these security requirements in mind, the following key BAM securities concepts will be covered in this chapter:

- Authentication
- Authorization
- **Secure Socket Layer (SSL)**

In this chapter, we will first discuss the topics related to client authentication, such as how to manage users and groups, and how to configure external LDAP servers for BAM. Then, you will learn how to manage security policies and application roles to control access to BAM resources. Finally, you will learn how to enable SSL for BAM.

Managing BAM authentication

BAM utilizes the authentication mechanism provided by the **Java Authentication and Authorization Service (JAAS)**, to validate identities of BAM users. JAAS is a Java security framework, which introduces the following key concepts:

- **Principal**: A Java object that represents an entity, such as a user, group, or role
- **Subject**: A Java object that represents a single entity that may contain multiple principals
- **Authentication**: The process of verifying a user's identity by using credentials, such as the username/password combination

When JAAS authenticates a subject, it first verifies its identity by checking its credential. If the credential is successfully verified, the authentication framework associates the credentials, as needed, with the subject, and then adds the principals to the subject.

Let's take a look at an object dump of a JAAS subject, which can be extracted from the diagnostic log file of the BAM Server.

```
BamSubject: BAM USER ID {2}
User{CLASS[weblogic.security.principal.WLSUserImpl] NAME[test1]}
Anonymous User{null}
Application
  Role{CLASS[oracle.security.jps.service.policystore.ApplicationRole]
  NAME[Report Architect] GUID[DBC02C10E55C11DE9F320B856DED04AD]
  APPLICATION[oracle-bam#11.1.1]}
Group{CLASS[oracle.security.jps.internal.core.principals.JpsAuthentic
  atedRoleImpl] NAME[authenticated-role] GUID[null]
  APPLICATION[null]}
```

`BamSubject` is a JAAS subject that represents a BAM user entity, which contains multiple principles. The LDAP user, `test1`, is a principal associated with this subject, and `Report Architect` is a principal that represents a role, defined in the `oracle-bam` application scope. The subject can also be propagated to other server components, so that credential validation is only required once.

Now, you should be familiar with the key JAAS concepts. To learn more about JAAS, refer to the official *JAAS Reference Guide* at the following URL:

http://download.oracle.com/javase/6/docs/technotes/guides/security/
jaas/JAASRefGuide.html

In the rest of the section, the following topics will be covered:

- Managing users and groups
- Using an external LDAP Server with BAM

Managing users and groups

Users and groups are stored in an identity store. To create a user in the WebLogic embedded LDAP Server, perform the following steps:

1. Log in to the WebLogic Server Administration Console. The URL is http://<hostname>:<port>/console, where <hostname> is the hostname of the Administration Server, and <port> is the HTTP listening port on the Administration Server (default is 7001).

2. In the **Domain Structure** pane, click on **Security Realms**.

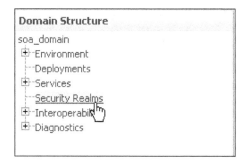

3. Click on myrealm in the **Realms** table.

4. In the **Settings** for the myrealm section, click on the **Users** and **Groups** tab, then click on the Users tab.

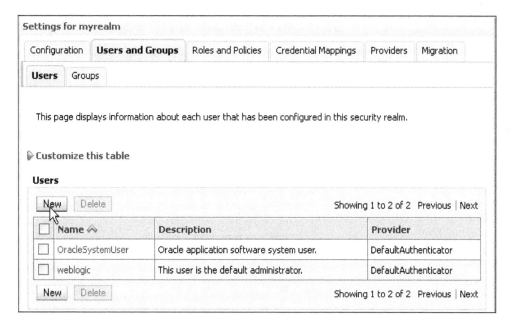

5. Click on **New**. If the WebLogic Server is started in the production mode, you need to click on the **Lock & Edit** button in the **Change Center** pane, before clicking on **New**.

6. In the **Create a New User** pane, enter the following key information:
   ○ **Name**: Specify the username, for example, test1.
   ○ **Provider**: Choose an authentication provider that connects to an identity store where users reside. Select the default provider (**DefaultAuthenticator**).
   ○ **Password**: Enter the password for the user.

7. Click on **OK**. A new user test1 is created and shown in the **Users** table.

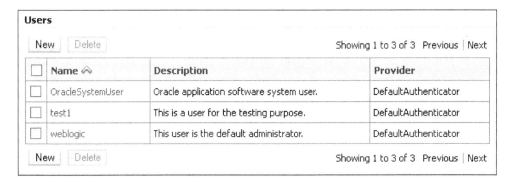

You can create a user group in the WebLogic Server console as well, by following the similar steps for creating a user. The key difference is that you need to click on the **New** button in the **Groups** tab, instead of the **Users** tab, and then specify the group name and an authentication provider.

Now if you enter the test1 user that you just created to log into the BAM start page (http://<hostname>:<port>/OracleBAM), you will see that all the buttons are disabled as shown in the following screenshot:

This is an expected behavior, as the user is not yet granted the proper permissions to access these BAM Web applications. The topic around user permissions will be covered later.

Using an external LDAP server with BAM

By default, users and groups are managed in the WebLogic embedded in the LDAP Server. However, in many cases, a third-party LDAP Server is used as the centralized identity store. In this section, you will learn how to configure BAM to use an external LDAP Server (for example, iPlanet LDAP Server) to validate users.

Creating a new Authentication provider

An **Authentication provider** is a security provider that is used to validate user identities. A WebLogic Server security realm can include one or more Authentication providers, each of which are designed to access different identity stores.

The `DefaultAuthenticator` is the default Weblogic Authentication provider. To use an external LDAP Server (for example, iPlanet LDAP Server) to authenticate users, you need to configure a separate Authentication provider, which connects to the LDAP Server. The steps are described as follows:

1. Log in to the WebLogic Server Administration Console. In the **Domain Structure** pane, click on **Security Realms**.

2. Click on `myrealm` in the **Realms** table.

3. In the **Settings** for `myrealm` section, click on the **Providers** tab, and then the **Authentication** tab.

4. Click on **New** in the **Authentication Providers** table.

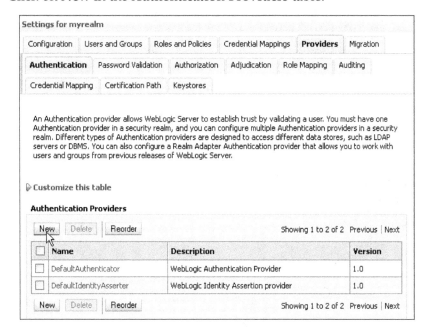

5. Specify the **name** and the **type** for the **Authentication Provider**. For example, enter `IPlanetAuthenticator` for the **name**, and then choose the **type** **IPlanetAuthenticator** for iPlanet LDAP Server.

6. Click on **OK**. The new Authentication provider appears in the **Authentication Providers** table.

7. Click on the provider in the table. A provider setting screen appears.

8. Click on the **Provider Specific** tab, and enter the following information:

    ○ **Host**: Enter the hostname or IP address for the LDAP Server.

    ○ **Port**: Enter the listening port for the LDAP Server.

    ○ **Principal**: Specify the **Distinguished Name (DN)** of the LDAP user that the Authentication provider uses to connect to the LDAP Server. For example, enter `cn=Directory Manager`.

    ○ **Credential**: Enter the password for the principal.

    ○ **Confirm Credential**: Enter the password again.

    ○ **User Base DN**: Specify the DN of the LDAP entry that contains users. For example, enter `ou=People,dc=mybookstore,dc=com`.

    ○ **User Name Attribute**: Enter the attribute that specifies the name of a LDAP user. `uid` is the default username attribute for the iPlanet LDAP Server.

    ○ **Use Retrieved User Name as Principal**: Select this option to ensure that the username retrieved from the LDAP Server is used as the principal in the subject.

    ○ **Group Base DN**: Specify the DN of the LDAP entry, which contains user groups. For example, enter the following:

      `ou=Groups,dc=mybookstore,dc=com`.

    ○ **SSLEnabled**: Specify whether SSL should be used to communicate with the LDAP Server. By default, this option is not selected.

9. Leave the other attributes unchanged, and then click on **Save**.

10. Click on the **Common** tab, and then choose **SUFFICIENT** from the list for the **Control Flag** attribute.

11. Click on **Save**.

12. Now in the **Authentication** tab, you should see the new **IplanetAuthenticator** provider, as shown in the following screenshot:

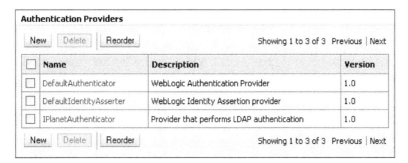

13. To make the changes take effect, you have to restart both the WebLogic Admin Server and the BAM Managed Server.

It is a best practice to set the **Control Flag** attribute to **SUFFICIENT** for each Authentication provider, if two or more Authentication providers are required in one security realm. **Oracle Security Platform Services (OPSS)**, the underlying security framework for BAM, iterates the list of the Authentication providers to perform user validations. In this case, any successful validation in one provider sufficiently determines the result. Only the failed authentication causes the validation to move forward to the next authenticator in the list.

Reordering Authentication providers

On the earlier releases of BAM 11gR1, for example PS1 or PS2, you need to reorder the Authentication providers, so that the LDAP-based security provider that you created earlier appears on the top of the list. However, from 11.1.1.4 (PS3) onwards, it is not needed, as OPSS begins to support multiple Authentication providers, which can be in any sequence.

On the 11.1.1.2 and the 11.1.1.3 releases, OPSS only supports authorization against the first entry in the list of providers. Therefore, if you would like to log in as the user from another Authentication provider, you have to reorder the authentication provider to the top of the list.

To reorder Authentication providers, you can simply click on **Reorder** in the **Authentication Providers** table in the **Authentication** tab, and then click on the arrow buttons to change the order.

Performing BAM specific configuration

BAM maintains its own security information, such as users, roles, permissions, and so on, in the repository. When a user successfully logs into the BAM start page, the user login information will be registered in the repository (the SysIterUser table). As part of the housekeeping process, a background thread runs every five minutes, by default, to check users and groups in BAM, to see whether they are still valid in the Authentication provider.

When a user is first registered in the SysIterUser table in the BAM schema, the **Inactive** field is set to 0, which indicates it is an active user. If users cannot be validated in the list of Authentication providers, the periodical housekeeping process will fail, and will consequently mark the user as inactive (the **Inactive** field is set to 1). If this happens, you will see the following error message: BAM-00404: Authentication failed. User is marked inactive when attempting to login.. To resolve this problem, you need to run the following SQL statement, which is used to reset the BAM user registration:

```
UPDATE "SysIterUser"
  SET "SysIterUser"."GUID" = NULL,
  "SysIterUser"."Inactive" = NULL;
```

> It is recommended to create the OracleSystemUser user in the user base DN in the LDAP Server. OracleSystemUser is an internal user used to perform internal housekeeping operations in the BAM Server.

Managing BAM authorization

Authorization is the process of determining what permissions a user can have when accessing protected resources. Oracle BAM uses the policy-based mechanism to achieve authorization. In this section, you will learn how to manage BAM authorization, in particular, how to manage application roles and policies.

Managing application roles

An **application role** is a virtual group defined in a centralized policy store, which is typically mapped to certain permissions that control the access of protected application resources. An application role contains members that can be users or groups defined in an LDAP Server, or another application role.

Granting permissions to application roles instead of physical users or groups, allows you to decouple the application-level permissions with principals defined in an identity store. Using application roles provides flexibility and ease of management. For example, suppose that you want to grant a number of permissions to a new user/group in the LDAP Server. You can simply add the user/group to the membership of the pre-defined application roles, without the need to understand the application-specific permission details.

BAM defines the following application roles in its default policy store, which is file-based and located in the `<WLS_BAM_Domain>/config/fmwconfig/system-jazn-data.xml` URL, where `<WLS_BAM_Domain>` is the WebLogic Server domain for BAM.

- `Administrator`: An administrator role that has full access to all BAM Server components and the BAM web applications
- `Report Architect`: A role that has the permission for creating data objects and reports
- `Report Creator`: A role that has the permission for creating reports
- `Report Viewer`: A role that has the permission for viewing reports

An example of the `Administrator` role looks as follows:

```
<app-role>
    <name>Administrator</name>
    <display-name>Has access to all features.</display-name>
    <guid>F4CEE940299D11E0AF7E8558D9E70321</guid>
    <class>
  oracle.security.jps.service.policystore.ApplicationRole
</class>
    <members>
    <member>
      <class>weblogic.security.principal.WLSGroupImpl</class>
      <name>Administrators</name>
    </member>
    <member>
      <class>weblogic.security.principal.WLSGroupImpl</class>
      <name>BamAdministrators</name>
    </member>
    <member>
      <class>weblogic.security.principal.WLSUserImpl</class>
      <name>OracleSystemUser</name>
    </member>
      </members>
</app-role>
```

As you can see, the Administrator application role is the implementation of the oracle.security.jps.service.policystore.ApplicationRole class, and contains the following members:

- Administrators: A group defined in either the WebLogic-embedded LDAP server, or an external LDAP Server

- BamAdministrators: A pre-configured group in the WebLogic-embedded LDAP Server

- OracleSystemUser: A BAM internal user defined in the WebLogic-embedded LDAP Server

To become a member of this specific role, you can add a user or a group to either the existing groups (Adminsitrators or BamAdministrators) defined in the LDAP Server or the application role explicitly. Managing users and groups in an LDAP Server is beyond the scope of this book. In the following section, you will learn how to add a user or group to an application role.

Adding a new user or group to an application role

Application roles are managed in the **Enterprise Manager Fusion Middleware Control**. To add a new user or group to an application role, perform the following steps:

1. Log in to the Enterprise Manager 11g Fusion Middleware Control. The URL is http://<hostname>:<port>/em.

2. Expand the **BAM** node in the farm for the SOA domain, and then click on **OracleBamServer**.

3. In the **OracleBamServer** pane, select **BAM Server | Security | Application Roles**. The **Application Roles** page appears.

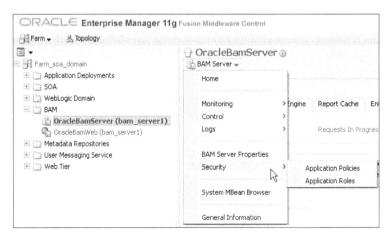

4. Click on the **Search application roles** icon. All the roles and their members are listed in the following table:

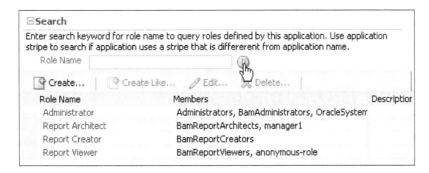

5. Click on a role name to edit its members. For example, click on the **Administrator** role.

6. Now, you can map the role to the users or the groups defined in the LDAP Server. For example, click on **Add User**, then select test1 from the **Available Users** list, and move it to the **Select Users** list.

7. Click on **OK**. The user becomes a new member of this role.

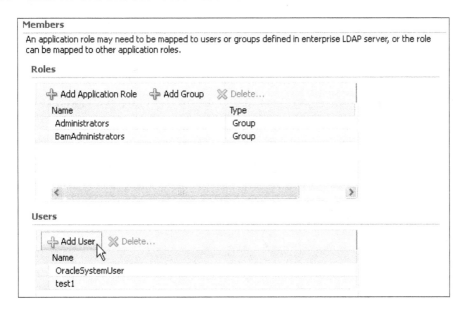

8. Now, if you attempt to log in to the BAM start page using the test1 user, you should be able to view the start page, which allows you to access all the BAM web applications.

The pre-defined BAM application roles should suffice in most scenarios. If you need more fine-grained access to the protected resources in BAM, you can create a new application role in the **Application Roles** page, and grant specific permissions to this role.

Managing BAM policies

Application policies are the JAAS policies that define the mapping rules between principals (users, groups, or application roles) and permissions for accessing protected resources.

First of all, let's take a look at the pre-defined permissions in BAM, as follows:

- `Administrator`: A permission that allows users to access the BAM Administrator
- `CreateDataObject`: A permission that allows users to create Data Objects
- `ActiveViewer`: A permission that allows users to access the BAM Active Viewer
- `ActiveStudio`: A permission that allows users to access the BAM Active Studio
- `Architect`: A permission that allows users to access the BAM Architect
- `CreateReport`: A permission that allows users to create reports
- `CreateAlertRule`: A permission that allows users to create alert rules
- `EmailRenderedReport`: A permission that allows users to e-mail rendered reports

Policies are defined in a **policy store**. The default policy store in BAM is a file-based policy store, which is `<WLS_BAM_Domain>/config/fmwconfig/system-jazn-data.xml`. The default policies defined in the policy store are the permissions granted to the pre-configured BAM application roles (`Administrator`, `Report Architect`, `Report Creator`, and `Report Viewer`). A sample policy is as follows:

```
<grant>
    <grantee>
      <principals>
        <principal>
        <class>
          oracle.security.jps.service.policystore.ApplicationRole
        </class>
          <name>Report Creator</name>
```

```
        <guid>F4CFAC91299D11E0AF7E8558D9E70321</guid>
      </principal>
    </principals>
  </grantee>
    <permissions>
    <permission>
      <class>oracle.bam.common.security.BAMPermission</class>
      <name>ActiveViewer</name>
    </permission>
    <permission>
      <class>oracle.bam.common.security.BAMPermission</class>
      <name>ActiveStudio</name>
    </permission>
    <permission>
      <class>oracle.bam.common.security.BAMPermission</class>
      <name>CreateReport</name>
    </permission>
    <permission>
      <class>oracle.bam.common.security.BAMPermission</class>
      <name>CreateAlertRule</name>
    </permission>
    <permission>
      <class>oracle.bam.common.security.BAMPermission</class>
      <name>EmailRenderedReport</name>
    </permission>
    </permissions>
  </grant>
```

As you can see, the `Report Creator` application role is granted the `ActiveViewer`, `ActiveStudio`, `CreateReport`, `CreateAlertRule`, and `EmailRenderedReport` permissions.

It is not recommended to modify the default policies. However, you are allowed to add your own policy, by granting proper permissions to your own application roles. The key steps for creating a policy are as follows:

1. In the EM console, expand the **BAM** node in the farm for the SOA domain, and then click on **OracleBamServer**.

2. In the **OracleBamServer** pane, select **BAM Server | Security | Application Policies**. The **Application Policies** page appears.

3. Click on **Create**.

4. In the **Grant Details** page, click on **Add** to add permissions, and then click on **Add Application Role** to add a `grantee`.

5. Click on **OK**. The new policy is successfully defined. You can search and view the policy either in the **Application Policies** page in the EM console, or in the policy store (for example, the `system-jazn-data.xml file`).

> You can create a policy by granting permissions to specific users or groups, instead of application roles. However, this tight association between physical users/groups and permissions is not recommended.

Configuring SSL for BAM

Secure Socket Layer (SSL) protocol allows WebLogic Server and its clients to communicate over a secure connection. As Oracle BAM is a Java enterprise application running on WebLogic Server, it utilizes the WebLogic Server SSL configuration to enforce the secure communications between BAM and its clients.

To configure SSL for BAM, you need to complete the following steps:

1. Prepare a server certificate.
2. Configure SSL for WebLogic Server.
3. Disable hostname verification (optional).

4. Enable SSL for BAM.

5. Enable SSL for `ICommand`.

Preparing a server certificate

To use the SSL, an application server must have an associated certificate, which allows the client to authenticate the server during the SSL hand-shake. One popular tool that can be used to set up a digital certificate is `keytool`, a key and certificate management utility that ships with the Java SDK.

The following steps demonstrate how to use `keytool` to create a `public-private` key pair and a self-signed certificate for a principal:

1. Generate a key pair in the identity key store `identity.jks`.

   ```
   $JAVA_HOME/bin/keytool -genkey -alias <alias> -keyalg RSA -keypass
   <password> -keystore identity.jks -storepass <storepass> -validity
   365
   ```

2. Enter the server name, organizational unit, organization, locality, state, and country code when `keytool` prompts.

3. Export the self-signed certificate from the identity key store into the file `bam.cer`.

   ```
   $JAVA_HOME/bin/keytool -export -alias <alias> -file bam.cer
   -keystore identity.jks
   ```

4. Import the self-signed certificate into the trust store `trust.jks`.

   ```
   $JAVA_HOME/bin/keytool -import -alias <alias> -trustcacerts -file
   bam.cer -keystore trust.jks
   ```

To learn more about `keytool`, refer to the `keytool` documentation at the following URL:

`http://java.sun.com/j2se/1.5.0/docs/tooldocs/solaris/key-tool.html`

Configuring SSL for the WebLogic Server

Configuring SSL for the WebLogic Server can be done through the WebLogic Server Administration Console, and requires the `keystores` and `truststores`, which contain certificates and trusted CAs.

The EM console that is used to manage BAM is running on the Administration Server, which also requires secure communications with the Managed Server over SSL. Therefore, it is important to set up SSL on both the Administration Server and the Managed Server for BAM. Otherwise, SSL connections cannot be initialized.

To enable SSL for the WebLogic Server, perform the following steps:

1. Log in to the WebLogic Server Administration Console.

2. In the **Domain Structure** page, navigate to **Environment | Servers |** <BAM_ Server>. Note that <BAM_Server> is the name of the Managed Server for BAM, for example, bam_server1.

3. Click on the **Configuration** tab, and then click on the **Keystores** tab.

4. Click on **Change**, and then choose **Custom Identity and Custom Trust** from the list.

5. In the **Keystores** configuration page, enter the following information:
   - **Custom Identity Keystore**: Enter the full path of the identity store file (identity.jks)
   - **Custom Identity Keystore Type**: Enter jks
   - **Custom Identity Keystore Passphrase**: Enter the password for the key store
   - **Confirm Custom Identity Keystore Passphrase**: Enter the password again
   - **Custom Trust Keystore**: Enter the full path of the trust store file (trust.jks)
   - **Custom Trust Keystore Type**: Enter jks
   - **Custom Trust Keystore Passphrase**: Enter the password for the trust store
   - **Confirm Custom Trust Keystore Passphrase**: Enter the password again

6. Click on **Save**.

7. Click on the **SSL** tab, and enter the following information:
   - **Private Key Alias**: Enter the private key alias
   - **Private Key Passphrase**: Enter the private key password
   - **Confirm Private Key Passphrase**: Enter the password again

8. Click on **Save**.

9. Click the **General** tab and enter the following information:
   ◦ **SSL Listen Port Enabled**: Check this option.
   ◦ **SSL Listen Port**: Set the listen port for SSL. The default is `9002`.

10. Click on **Save**.

11. Repeat *steps 2* to *11* for configuring SSL on the Administration Server.

12. Restart the Administration Server and the Managed Server for BAM.

Disabling hostname verification (optional)

This step is only required if you have not set up the appropriate certificates to authenticate the different nodes with the Administration Server. For example, if you use the self-signed certificate, you have to disable hostname verification from both the Administration Server and the Managed Server for BAM.

 Disabling hostname verification is not recommended on production environments. This is only suggested for testing purposes. Hostname verification helps to prevent man-in-the-middle attacks.

Perform these steps to disable hostname verification:

1. Log in to the WebLogic Server Administration Console.

2. In the **Domain Structure** pane, navigate to **Environment | Servers | <Admin_Server>**. Note that <Admin_Server> is the name of the Administration Server.

3. Click on the **Configuration** tab, and then the **SSL** tab.

4. Click on **Advanced**.

5. Select **None** for the **Hostname Verification** field.

6. Click on **Save**.

7. Repeat *steps 2* to *6* for the <BAM_Server>.

Enabling SSL for BAM

Internally, BAM uses RMI for communications between different components. By default, RMI communications in WebLogic Server use the `t3` protocol, an optimized protocol for transporting data between the WebLogic Server components. For example, BAM Active Data Cache communicates with internal JMS topics using RMI through the `t3` protocol. BAM web applications invoke BAM Active Data Cache APIs through RMI (`t3`) as well.

 To enable SSL for these internal communications, BAM introduces a parameter called `BAMServerEnableSSO`, which can only be manually configured in the `BAMCommonConfig.xml` file. With SSL enabled, the communication protocol becomes `t3s`.

To set up this parameter, add the following configuration in the `<BAM_Domain>` / `config/fmwconfig/servers/<BAM_Server>/applications/oracle-bam_11.1.1/ config/BAMCommonConfig.xml` file, where `<BAM_Domain>` is the WebLogic domain name of the Managed Server for BAM, and `<BAM_Server>` is the name of the Managed Server.

```
<BAMServerEnableSSO>true</BAMServerEnableSSO>
```

Note that you have to restart the Managed Server for BAM to make the change take effect.

 Enabling SSL for BAM is not required if BAM is running on both SSL and non-SSL ports. However, if the SSL port is the only port enabled on the Managed Server for BAM, you have to enable SSL for BAM. Otherwise, the internal communication channel is broken.

Enabling SSL for ICommand

`ICommand` is a command-line utility that performs BAM operations, such as importing and exporting Data Objects. By default, `ICommand` interacts with BAM Active Data Cache through the `t3` protocol. You can enable SSL for `ICommand`, by setting its protocol to `t3s`.

To enable SSL for `ICommand`, set the following properties in the `<Oracle_Home>/ bam/config/BAMICommandConfig.xml` file, where `<Oracle_Home>` is the home directory for SOA:

```
<Communication_Protocol>t3s</Communication_Protocol>
```

Summary

In this chapter, you learned how to manage users, groups, application roles, and application policies to achieve BAM authentication and authorization. You also learned how to configure an external LDAP server and SSL for BAM, which are the most common requirements that we have seen in a BAM project.

Now, you should be ready to tackle the advanced BAM administration topics, such as migrations, **High Availability** (HA), troubleshooting, and ADF, which will be covered in the following chapters.

7
Migrating BAM to a Different Environment

In the development life cycle, it is very common to build different environments (development, testing, UAT, and production) to meet your business needs. Thus, the capability of moving data from one environment to another, smoothly and effectively, becomes critical for your business.

Building a new environment is the starting point for BAM data migration. You can either install Oracle BAM from scratch or clone an existing BAM installation. No matter what approach you take, the prerequisite is the installation of Oracle BAM schema in a database using the **Repository Creation Utility (RCU)**.

Installing schemas using RCU is beyond the scope of this book. For more information, refer to Oracle Fusion Middleware Repository Creation Utility User's Guide, which can be found in the Fusion Middleware documentation library. Note that the URL of this document varies among different releases. For example, on 11.1.1.6, the home page of RCU is `http://docs.oracle.com/cd/E23943_01/doc.1111/e14259/rcu.htm`.

This chapter discusses the technologies and best practices for performing BAM migration, and you will learn the following topics:

- Cloning Oracle BAM
- Performing BAM data migration using database commands
- Performing BAM data migration using `ICommand`

Cloning Oracle BAM

Cloning is the process of copying an existing environment to the same directory on a target system, while keeping its state (for example, topologies, configurations, application deployments, and so on) unchanged. Cloning simplifies the process of building identical environments on different hosts by copying all middleware components and their patches. It also provides an effective way for distributing BAM domain configurations among different environments.

The prerequisites for cloning Oracle BAM are as follows:

- Installing the Oracle BAM schema using RCU.
- Stopping the administration server and all managed servers running in the domain on the source host.
- On Unix/Linux, verifying if the `oraInst.loc` file exists in the `/etc` directory. If it is located in another directory, use the `-invPtrLoc` option with the `pasteBinary` script to specify the location. If the target host does not contain the file `oraInst.loc`, you must create the file that includes the `inventory_loc` and `inst_group` properties. For example, a sample of the `oraInst.loc` file looks as follows:

```
inventory_loc=/u01/app/oraInventory
inst_group=oinstall
```

To clone Oracle BAM, the following steps are performed:

1. Cloning a Middleware home.
2. Cloning the WebLogic Server domain for BAM.

Cloning a Middleware home

You can clone a Middleware home using the `copyBinary` and `pasteBinary` scripts located in the `<MW_HOME>/oracle_common/bin` directory.

Creating an archive of a Middleware home

Oracle Fusion Middleware provides the `copyBinary` script that can be used to create an archive of a Middleware home, which contains the WebLogic Server home, and one or more Oracle homes, such as SOA, BAM, HTTP server, and so on.

The syntax of the `copyBinary` script is as follows:

```
copyBinary -javaHome <JAVA_HOME>
            -archiveLoc <ARCHIVE_LOCATION>
            -sourceMWHomeLoc <MW_HOME>
```

Note that you need to replace the following variables with the actual values:

- `<JAVA_HOME>`: The absolute path of the Java home
- `<ARCHIVE_LOCATION>`: The absolute path of the archive file location
- `<MW_HOME>`: The source of the Fusion Middleware `home` directory

It is best practice to create a `sh` script on Unix/Linux, or a batch file on Windows to execute the `copyBinary` script. For example, the following `sh` script can be used to create the archive (`mw_clone.jar`) of the Middleware home, which is `/u01/app/oracle/product/fmw` on Unix/Linux:

```
#!/bin/sh
MW_HOME=/u01/app/oracle/product/fmw
export MW_HOME
ORACLE_COMMON_HOME=$MW_HOME/oracle_common
export ORACLE_COMMON_HOME
JAVA_HOME=$MW_HOME/jdk160_21
export JAVA_HOME
ARCHIVE_LOC=/home/samples/migration/files/mw_clone.jar
export ARCHIVE_LOC
$ORACLE_COMMON_HOME/bin/copyBinary.sh -javaHome $JAVA_HOME -archiveLoc
$ARCHIVE_LOC -sourceMWHomeLoc $MW_HOME
```

Copying required files

If you are cloning the Middleware home to a different host, copy the following files to the target system, and ensure that they are granted the `execute` permission:

- `ORACLE_COMMON_HOME/bin/pasteBinary.cmd` on Windows, or `ORACLE_COMMON_HOME/bin/pasteBinary.sh` on Unix/Linux
- `ORACLE_COMMON_HOME/jlib/cloningclient.jar`
- Your Middleware home archive file, for example, `/home/samples/migration/files/mw_clone.jar`

The pasteBinary script and cloningclient.jar file have to be copied to the same directory on the target system.

Extracting the archive in a target system

The pasteBinary script can be used to extract the files from the archive at a target host.

The syntax of the pasteBinary script is as follows:

```
pasteBinary -javaHome <JAVA_HOME>
            -archiveLoc <ARCHIVE_LOCATION>
            -targetMWHomeLoc <MW_HOME>
```

Note that you need to replace the following variables with the actual values:

- <JAVA_HOME>: The absolute path of the Java home (JDK 1.6.0 Update 4 or later release)
- <ARCHIVE_LOCATION>: The absolute path of the archive file location
- <MW_HOME>: The target Fusion Middleware home directory

For example, to apply the clone (mw_clone.jar) to the /u02/app/oracle/product/fmw directory, use the following sh script:

```
#!/bin/sh
MW_HOME=/u02/app/oracle/product/fmw
export MW_HOME
JAVA_HOME=/u01/app/oracle/product/fmw/jdk160_21
export JAVA_HOME
ARCHIVE_LOC=/home/samples/migration/files/mw_clone.jar
export ARCHIVE_LOC
./pasteBinary.sh -javaHome $JAVA_HOME -archiveLoc $ARCHIVE_LOC
-targetMWHomeLoc $MW_HOME
```

When specifying the target file path for the targetMWHomeLoc parameter, ensure that the file path does not exist, and has the write permission.

Cloning a WebLogic Server domain for BAM

Cloning a WebLogic Server domain for BAM enables you to obtain a snapshot of the BAM domain configuration, and then apply the snapshot to a different environment.

Creating an archive of a WebLogic Server domain for BAM

To create an archive of a WebLogic Server domain for BAM, use the `copyConfig` script in the `<MW_HOME>/oracle_common/bin` directory as follows:

```
copyConfig   -javaHome <JAVA_HOME>
             -archiveLoc <ARCHIVE_LOCATION>
             -sourceDomainLoc <DOMAIN_LOCATION>
             -sourceMWHomeLoc <MW_HOME>
             -domainHostName <HOSTNAME>
             -domainPortNum   <PORT>
             -domainAdminUserName <USERNAME>
             -domainAdminPassword <PASSWORD_FILE>
```

Note that you need to replace the following variables with the actual values:

- `<JAVA_HOME>`: The absolute path of the Java home
- `<ARCHIVE_LOCATION>`: The absolute path of the archive file location
- `<DOMAIN_LOCATION>`: The absolute path of the WebLogic Server domain for BAM
- `<MW_HOME>`: The source Fusion Middleware home directory
- `<HOSTNAME>`: The hostname of the administration server for the domain
- `<PORT>`: The listening port of the administration server for the domain
- `<USERNAME>`: The username of the domain administrator
- `<PASSWORD_FILE>`: The absolute path of the file containing the password for the domain administrator

> Before running the script, ensure that the administration server and all managed servers in the source Middleware home are started successfully. The `password` file that contains the clear text password should be maintained securely in the file system.

For example, to create an archive of the SOA/BAM domain (soa_domain) for the Middleware home (/u01/app/oracle/product/fmw), use the following sh script:

```sh
#!/bin/sh
MW_HOME=/u02/app/oracle/product/fmw
export MW_HOME
ORACLE_COMMON_HOME=$MW_HOME/oracle_common
export ORACLE_COMMON_HOME
JAVA_HOME=$MW_HOME/jdk160_21
export JAVA_HOME
ARCHIVE_LOC=/home/samples/migration/files/config_clone.jar
export ARCHIVE_LOC
$ORACLE_COMMON_HOME/bin/copyConfig.sh -javaHome $JAVA_HOME -archiveLoc
$ARCHIVE_LOC -sourceMWHomeLoc $MW_HOME -sourceDomainLoc $MW_HOME/user_
projects/domains/soa_domain -domainHostName myhostname -domainPortNum
7001 -domainAdminUserName weblogic -domainAdminPassword /home/oracle/
password.txt
```

Extracting move plans

A **move plan** is a migration property file that contains configurable information, which can be applied to the target system. For example, you can edit the move plan (moveplan.xml) to change the WebLogic Server instance start mode (DEVELOPMENT or PRODUCTION), its listening address, as well as other resource configurations, such as data sources, JMS, adapters, and so on.

First of all, you need to copy the archive file to the target system if you are cloning the BAM domain to a different host, and then, run the extractMovePlan script to extract the move plan from the archive. The script syntax is as follows:

```
extractMovePlan -javaHome <JAVA_HOME>
                -archiveLoc <ARCHIVE_LOCATION>
                -planDirLoc <PLAN_DIR>
```

Note that you need to replace the following variables with the actual values:

- <JAVA_HOME>: The absolute path of the Java home
- <ARCHIVE_LOCATION>: The absolute path of the archive file location
- <PLAN_DIR>: The absolute path of the directory that contains the move plans

For example, the following `sh` script extracts the move plans from the domain archive file (`config_clone.jar`) to the `/home/oracle/mybook/samples/migration/files/plans` directory on the target host:

```sh
#!/bin/sh
MW_HOME=/u02/app/oracle/product/fmw
export MW_HOME
ORACLE_COMMON_HOME=$MW_HOME/oracle_common
export ORACLE_COMMON_HOME
JAVA_HOME=$MW_HOME/jdk160_21
export JAVA_HOME
ARCHIVE_LOC=/home/samples/migration/files/config_clone.jar
export ARCHIVE_LOC
$ORACLE_COMMON_HOME/bin/extractMovePlan.sh -javaHome $JAVA_HOME
-archiveLoc $ARCHIVE_LOC -planDirLoc /home/oracle/mybook/samples/
migration/files/plans
```

> The directory specified for the `planDirLoc` property in the `extractMovePlan` script must not exist in the file system. However, its parent location must exist in the file system, and have the `write` permission. In the previous example, the `/home/oracle/mybook/samples/migration/files` directory should be present in the file system, but the `plans` sub-directory should not exist.

Editing move plans

Move plans are extracted and placed in the following directory structure:

- `<PLAN_DIR>/moveplan.xml`: The main move plan configuration file
- `<PLAN_DIR>/adapters`: The directory that contains sub plans for adapters
- `<PLAN_DIR>/composites`: The directory that contains sub plans for SOA composites
- `<PLAN_DIR>/deployment_plans`: The directory that contains sub plans for the soa-infra application

The main move plan (`moveplan.xml`) captures the key information in the `domain.xml` file for a particular WebLogic Server domain. So, you can modify the domain configurations, such as the server startup mode, data sources, authentication providers, and so on, and then apply the changes to the new domain on the target host.

As all the passwords are indirectly stored in the plan through password files, you must specify the absolute path of the location for every occurrence of the password filename in the `moveplan.xml` file. For example, for each data source, you need to specify the password file location as follows:

```
<configProperty>
  <name>Password File</name>
  <value>/home/oracle/password.txt</value>
  <itemMetadata>
    <dataType>STRING</dataType>
    <password>true</password>
    <scope>READ_WRITE</scope>
  </itemMetadata>
</configProperty>
```

Another important property in the move plan is the database connection URL, which is used by the data sources. For example, to change the JDBC connection URLs of the data sources used by SOA and BAM components, edit the `moveplan.xml` file as follows:

```
<configProperty>
  <name>Url</name>
  <value>jdbc:oracle:thin:@myDBHost:1521:SID</value>
  <itemMetadata>
      <dataType>STRING</dataType>
      <scope>READ_WRITE</scope>
  </itemMetadata>
</configProperty>
```

You can also modify the configuration of adapters (database adapters, JMS adapters, BAM adapters, and so on), by editing the corresponding adapter plan in the `<PLAN_DIR>/adapters` directory. To learn more about plan properties, refer to the *Oracle Fusion Middleware Administrator's* guide.

> You can only modify the plan properties with the scope of `READ_WRITE`. Changing the properties with the scope of `READ_ONLY` will cause script run-time errors.

Extracting the archive in a target system

On the target host, extract the files from the archive using the `pasteConfig` script:

```
pasteConfig   -javaHome <JAVA_HOME>

              -archiveLoc <ARCHIVE_LOCATION>

              -targetDomainLoc <DOMAIN_LOC>

              -targetMWHomeLoc <MW_HOME>

              -movePlanLoc <PLAN_DIR>

              -domainAdminPassword <PASSWORD>
```

For example, to extract the archive of the BAM domain to a new domain, `<MW_HOME>/user_projects/domains/soa_domain`, use the following `sh` script:

```
#!/bin/sh
MW_HOME=/u02/app/oracle/product/fmw
export MW_HOME
ORACLE_COMMON_HOME=$MW_HOME/oracle_common
export ORACLE_COMMON_HOME
JAVA_HOME=$MW_HOME/jdk160_21
export JAVA_HOME
ARCHIVE_LOC=/home/samples/migration/files/config_clone.jar
export ARCHIVE_LOC
DOMAIN_LOC=$MW_HOME/user_projects/domains/soa_domain
export DOMAIN_LOC
$ORACLE_COMMON_HOME/bin/pasteConfig.sh -javaHome $JAVA_HOME -archiveLoc
$ARCHIVE_LOC -movePlanLoc /home/oracle/mybook/samples/migration/files/
plans/moveplan.xml -targetDomainLoc $DOMAIN_LOC -targetMWHomeLoc $MW_HOME
-domainAdminPassword /home/oracle/password.txt
```

> All the move plans are ready-to-use if the Middleware home on the target host is the same as the source host. If you choose to clone the Middleware home to a different directory on the target host, you need to manually edit the `config-root` property in all the plans under the `<PLAN_DIR>/adapters` directory and the `<PLAN_DIR>/deployment_plans` directory as follows:
>
> ```
> <config-root><MW_HOME>/Oracle_SOA1/soa/connectors/
> plan</config-root>
> ```

Performing additional configurations and testing

As you saw in the *Cloning a Middleware home* and the *Cloning a WebLogic Server domain for BAM* sections, the cloning scripts copy the configurations of the Middleware home and the WebLogic Server domain for BAM. However, these scripts do not help to copy BAM specific configurations to a new environment. Therefore, you should perform additional configuration steps as follows:

1. Configuring a security store or a policy store for BAM, if needed (optional).
2. Setting up BAM properties using the EM console (optional).

You will learn about these BAM-specific configurations in detail in the next chapter, along with other **High Availability** (**HA**)-related topics.

Now, the environment should be ready for testing. To verify the cloned environment, perform the following steps:

1. Start the administration server and the managed server for BAM.
2. Try to log in to the BAM start page, and access all the BAM web applications.
3. If you can successfully access these applications, you can move on to the next section to conduct the data migration tasks.

Performing data migration

After you have successfully created a new environment for Oracle BAM, it is time to move BAM data to the environment. You can use either the low-level database commands or ICommand, a BAM utility to achieve this goal.

Migrating BAM data using database commands

BAM stores its artifacts (Data Objects, reports, folders, and so on) and metadata in a database. Therefore, it is practical to perform data migration by using database commands to move raw data directly to a different environment. Though BAM supports Oracle Database, IBM DB2, and Microsoft SQLServer, this section only covers the usage of Oracle database commands to achieve data migration.

The `expdp` database command can be used to export the database schema for BAM on the source host, while the `impdp` command is for importing the dump file to the database on the target host. Because these are the low-level database methods, this approach is more suitable in the case of the initial data migration to a fresh installation, or cloning a database schema that does not contain any business data yet.

To perform BAM data migration using Oracle Database commands, do the following:

1. Connect to the BAM database as the `sys` user.

   ```
   sqlplus sys/password as sysdba
   ```

2. Execute the following SQL commands to create a database directory named `dmpdir`:

   ```
   SQL> CREATE DIRECTORY dmpdir AS '<DIR>';

   SQL> GRANT read, write ON DIRECTORY dmpdir TO <BAM_SCHEMA_NAME>;
   ```

   When using these commands, replace the following variables:

   - `<DIR>`: The directory location on the file system of the database server, for example, `/home/oracle/migration`

   - `<BAM_SCHEMA_NAME>`: The database schema name for Oracle BAM, for example, `dev_orabam`

3. Shut down the administration server and all the managed servers.

4. Execute the following Oracle database command to export the database schema of Oracle BAM.

   ```
   ORACLE_HOME/bin/expdp <BAM_SCHEMA_NAME> DIRECTORY=dmpdir
   SCHEMAS=<BAM_SCHEMA_NAME> DUMPFILE=orabam.dmp
   ```

5. Replace the `<BAM_SCHEMA_NAME>` with the Oracle BAM schema name.

6. Copy the `dump` file to the target node.

7. Create a target schema on the target node, and then repeat *steps 1* and *2* to create the database directory named `dmpdir` on the target node.

8. Import the database schema for Oracle BAM that you exported earlier using the following command:

```
ORACLE_HOME/bin/impdp system/<PASSWORD>  DIRECTORY=dmpdir REMAP_
SCHEMA=<SOURCE_SCHEMA>:<TARGET_SCHEMA> DUMPFILE=orabam.dmp
```

In this command, replace the following variables with the actual values:

   ° `<PASSWORD>`: The password for the system user

   ° `<SOURCE_SCHEMA>`: The database schema name for Oracle BAM on the source node, for example, `dev_orabam`

   ° `<TARGET_SCHEMA>`: The database schema name for Oracle BAM, for example, `prod_orabam`

9. Now, all the BAM artifacts, such as data objects, folders, reports, alerts, and so on, are moved to the new environment. Restart the managed server for BAM.

Migrating BAM data using ICommand

The `expdp` and `impdp` database commands can be used to move raw BAM data to a different environment. However, they don't have the capability of controlling what BAM artifacts should be moved to the target database, or the history of the BAM metadata. Thus, in many cases, it is more flexible and convenient to utilize the BAM `ICommand` utility to perform data migration tasks for BAM.

In this section, you will learn how to use `ICommand` to migrate the `Bookstore Demo` application to a different environment.

Using the EXPORT command

On the source host, execute the following commands to export BAM artifacts (Data Objects, reports, rules, EMS, and EDS) to the corresponding XML files:

```
icommand -CMD EXPORT -TYPE DATAOBJECT -ALL 1 -DEPENDENCIES 1 -FILE
DataObjects.xml

icommand -CMD EXPORT -TYPE REPORT -ALL 1 -FILE Reports.xml

icommand -CMD EXPORT -TYPE RULE -ALL 1 -FILE Rules.xml

icommand -CMD EXPORT -TYPE EMS -ALL 1 -FILE EMS.xml

icommand -CMD EXPORT -TYPE EDS -ALL 1 -FILE EDS.xml
```

The usage of the aforementioned Icommand parameters is described as follows:

- CMD: This parameter is used to specify the command name. Set it to EXPORT when exporting BAM artifacts to a file, and set it to IMPORT when importing BAM artifacts from a file.

- TYPE: This parameter is used to specify the type of a BAM artifact (for example, DATAOBJECT, REPORT, RULE, EMS, EDS, and so on).

- ALL: This parameter is used to specify the set of the artifacts. This parameter is set to 0, by default. Set it to 1, if you want to perform an operation on all the artifacts with the specified type.

- DEPENDENCIES: This parameter is used only when the DATAOBJECT type is specified. Set it to 1, if you want to preserve the dependencies among the Data Objects.

- FILE: This parameter is used to specify the filename, which should be .xml for the import or the export operations.

To merge the export files into a single file, use the APPEND, HEADER, and FOOTER parameters as follows:

```
icommand -CMD EXPORT -TYPE DATAOBJECT -ALL 1 -DEPENDENCIES 1 -FILE
export.xml -HEADER 1 -FOOTER 0

icommand -CMD EXPORT -TYPE REPORT -ALL 1 -FILE export.xml -APPEND 1
-HEADER 0 -FOOTER 0

icommand -CMD EXPORT -TYPE RULE -ALL 1 -FILE export.xml -APPEND 1 -HEADER
0 -FOOTER 0

icommand -CMD EXPORT -TYPE EMS -ALL 1 -FILE export.xml -APPEND 1 -HEADER
0 -FOOTER 0

icommand -CMD EXPORT -TYPE EDS -ALL 1 -FILE export.xml -APPEND 1 -HEADER
0 -FOOTER 1
```

The HEADER flag specifies whether the XML header information is written to the front of the export file. Similarly, the FOOTER flag determines if the footer information should be added to the end of the export file. As you have only one header and footer in the export file, set the HEADER flag to 1 in the first ICommand statement, and set the FOOTER flag to 1 in the last ICommand statement. The APPEND flag controls whether the contents will be appended to an existing file or not.

The previous example exports all Data Objects and reports to the export file. However, if you only want to move your application-specific data (for example, the Bookstore Demo application data) to a new environment, use the following scripts:

```
#!/bin/sh

MW_HOME=/u03/app/ofm11114/Middleware export MW_HOME
```

```
BAM_HOME=$MW_HOME/Oracle_SOA1/bam export BAM_HOME
JAVA_HOME=$MW_HOME/jdk160_21 export JAVA_HOME
EXPORT_FILE=/home/samples/icommand/files/ch7export.xml
export EXPORT_FILE

#Export Data Objects
$BAM_HOME/bin/icommand -CMD EXPORT -NAME "/public/DataObject/
BookstoreDemo/Customer"  -FILE "$EXPORT_FILE" -HEADER 1 -FOOTER 0
$BAM_HOME/bin/icommand -CMD EXPORT -NAME "/public/DataObject/
BookstoreDemo/Order_Status" -FILE "$EXPORT_FILE" -APPEND 1 -HEADER 0
-FOOTER 0
$BAM_HOME/bin/icommand -CMD EXPORT -NAME "/public/DataObject/
BookstoreDemo/Order_Item" -FILE "$EXPORT_FILE" -APPEND 1 -HEADER 0
-FOOTER 0
$BAM_HOME/bin/icommand -CMD EXPORT -NAME "/public/DataObject/
BookstoreDemo/Order" -FILE "$EXPORT_FILE" -APPEND 1 -HEADER 0 -FOOTER 0

#Export Reports
$BAM_HOME/bin/icommand -CMD EXPORT -NAME "/public/Report/BookstoreDemo/
OrderTrackingReport" -TYPE REPORT -FILE "$EXPORT_FILE" -APPEND 1 -HEADER
0 -FOOTER 0

#Export EMS
$BAM_HOME/bin/icommand -CMD EXPORT -ALL 1 -TYPE EMS -FILE "$EXPORT_FILE"
-APPEND 1 -HEADER 0 -FOOTER 1
```

This script only exports the Bookstore application-related data to a single file called ch7export.xml. When specifying the name of a particular Data Object, use the full path, which is /public/DataObject/<Location>/<Data_Object_Name>. You can find the values for <Location> and <Data_Object_Name> in the BAM Architect Web application as shown in the next screenshot. Similarly, for a public report, the name should be /public/Report/<Report_Folder>/<Report_Name>.

In many cases, the parameter –CONTENT 0 is often used in the export command to prevent business data from being copied to other environments.

Using the IMPORT command

Once you have the export files in place, you can use the IMPORT command to import BAM data to your target environment for BAM.

The syntax of the IMPORT command is as follows:

- On Windows:

  ```
  icommand.bat -CMD IMPORT -FILE <EXPORT_FILE>
  ```

- On Unix/Linux:

  ```
  icommand -CMD IMPORT -FILE <EXPORT_FILE>
  ```

The following example demonstrates how to use a sh script to import BAM data:

```
#!/bin/sh
MW_HOME=/u03/app/ofm11114/Middleware export MW_HOME
BAM_HOME=$MW_HOME/Oracle_SOA1/bam export BAM_HOME
JAVA_HOME=$MW_HOME/jdk160_21 export JAVA_HOME
EXPORT_FILE=/home/oracle/mybook/samples/icommand/files/ch7export.xml
export EXPORT_FILE

#Clean the environment
$BAM_HOME/bin/icommand -CMD DELETE -TYPE EMS -ALL 1
$BAM_HOME/bin/icommand -CMD DELETE -TYPE DATAOBJECT -NAME "/public/
DataObject/BookstoreDemo/Order"
$BAM_HOME/bin/icommand -CMD DELETE -TYPE DATAOBJECT -NAME "/public/
DataObject/BookstoreDemo/Order_Item"
$BAM_HOME/bin/icommand -CMD DELETE -TYPE DATAOBJECT -NAME "/public/
DataObject/BookstoreDemo/Order_Status"
$BAM_HOME/bin/icommand -CMD DELETE -TYPE DATAOBJECT -NAME "/public/
DataObject/BookstoreDemo/Customer"
$BAM_HOME/bin/icommand -CMD DELETE -TYPE FOLDER -NAME "/public/
DataObject/BookstoreDemo"
$BAM_HOME/bin/icommand -CMD DELETE -TYPE REPORT -NAME "/public/Report/
BookstoreDemo/OrderTrackingReport"

#Import BAM artifacts
$BAM_HOME/bin/icommand -CMD IMPORT -FILE "$EXPORT_FILE"
```

As you can see in this example, the DELETE commands are executed before the IMPORT command to clean the environment. Due to the dependencies, it is best practice to order the DELETE commands in the sequence of EMS, Data Objects, lookup Data Objects, folders, and reports.

Performing additional configurations

After importing an EMS or **External Data Sources** (**EDS**) to a new environment, it is required to review and change its configuration accordingly through the BAM Architect web application.

After you perform these additional steps, the BAM migration task completes. You should be able to perform testing based on your requirements from now on.

Summary

In this chapter, you learned the technologies and best practices of cloning Oracle BAM, and performing data migrations for BAM. Cloning is an important feature, which allows you to move a working environment to other hosts without going through installing, patching, and configurations, and you may find that it is useful in your own project.

The steps and instructions provided in this chapter are suitable for creating an environment with the same topology or domain structure. If you want to build an environment for **High Availability** (**HA**), go through the next chapter that focuses on HA topics, such as BAM HA configuration, server migrations, and so on.

8

Configuring High Availability for BAM

To reinforce enterprise-level security and maximize **High Availability (HA)**, an enterprise deployment topology typically requires a multi-tier architecture that is composed of the Client tier, the Web tier, the Application Server tier, and the Database tier. Each tier is a complete administration unit, which allows separate installation and configuration without affecting the other tiers.

A typical BAM HA topology is shown in the following diagram. As you can see, each tier can have its own HA configuration, which ensures that there is no single point of failure in the entire architecture:

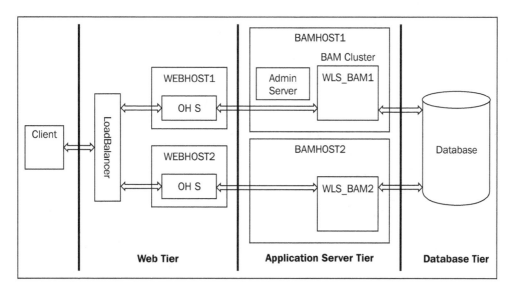

For simplicity, this chapter only covers the HA configuration for Oracle BAM in the Application Server tier. After the completion of the BAM HA configuration, you are free to extend your current topology to include a load balancer, or even a Web Server in the Web tier.

You will learn the following topics in this chapter:

- Preparing your HA environment
- Configuring a WebLogic Server domain for BAM HA
- Configuring server migration

Preparing your HA environment

Setting up your environment, such as operating systems, databases, networking, storages, and so on, is the prerequisite for configuring your HA environment for BAM. In this section, you will learn how to perform these tasks to complete the setup of your environment.

Configuring databases

Oracle BAM stores its metadata and business transactional data in a repository, which requires a relational database (Oracle Database, IBM DB2, or Microsoft SQL Server). However, using Oracle Database is a common practice, especially in an HA environment. Throughout this chapter, Oracle Database will be used to illustrate the HA configuration details.

Installing database schemas for SOA/BAM

To install database schemas for SOA/BAM in an existing database, perform the following steps:

1. Ensure that your Oracle database meets the following requirements before continuing to the next step:
    - Oracle Database 10.2.0.4 or above
    - Oracle Database 11.1.0.7 or above
    - Oracle Database 11.2.0.1 or above

2. To install the BAM schema, run the **Repository Creation Utility (RCU)**, which can be found in the SOA (BAM) installation package.

   ```
   RCU_HOME/bin/rcu
   ```

3. In the **Database Connection Details** screen, provide the connection details.

4. In the **Select Components** screen, select **SOA and BPM Infrastructure**, and click on **Next**.

5. Complete the rest of the steps to set up passwords, and map table spaces.

Setting up database parameters

The `processes` parameter on an Oracle database instance represents the maximal number of open sessions (active database connections) allowed at the database side. As Oracle SOA Suite and Oracle BAM use their dedicated data sources to connect to the backend database, it is important to set the `processes` parameter to an appropriate value, so that SOA/BAM can always obtain database connections if needed.

To set this parameter, perform the following steps:

1. Connect to the database server as the `sys` user or a user with the DBA role.

2. Run the following Oracle database command to determine the number of processes for the database instance:

   ```
   SQL> SHOW PARAMETER processes;
   ```

3. Determine the appropriate value for the `processes` parameter. The recommended setting of the `processes` parameter is dependent on the Fusion Middleware components used in your system. For example, if you are using BAM, this parameter should be set to `100` or above. If you are using both SOA and BAM, it is recommended to set this parameter to `400` or above.

4. To change the value of this parameter, run the following Oracle command, and then restart the database:

   ```
   SQL> ALTER SYSTEM SET processes=400 SCOPE=SPFILE
   ```

Granting transactional recovery privileges

You need to grant appropriate transaction recovery privileges to the BAM schema, so that the WebLogic Server transaction manager can handle transaction recoveries in case of WebLogic Server failure.

To grant privileges to the BAM schema for the transaction recovery purpose, execute the following commands:

```
SQL> Grant select on sys.dba_pending_transactions to <bam_schema>;
Grant succeeded.
```

```
SQL> Grant force any transaction to <bam_schema>;

Grant succeeded.
```

Grant these privileges to the SOA schema if SOA is used in your system.

Choosing the recommended WebLogic Server topology

A Weblogic Server topology represents a domain architecture that defines the deployment of WebLogic Server components, such as the Administration Server, Managed Servers, clusters, and machines. The following diagram depicts the recommended domain architecture for Oracle BAM:

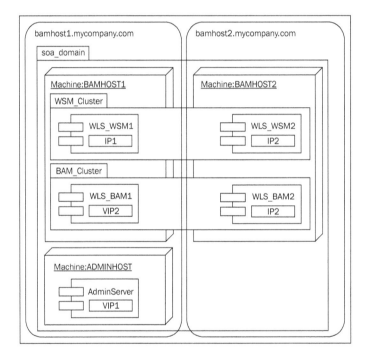

This domain architecture contains the following servers:

- `AdminServer`: This is the Administration Server assigned to `ADMINHOST`, which is the logical machine defined in the domain. The `AdminServer` instance runs on the `bamhost1.mycompany.com` host, while its listen address should be `adminvhn.mycompany.com` that resolves to `VIP1`.

- `WLS_WSM1`: This is the Managed Server that hosts the Web Service Manager. It listens on the physical IP (`IP1`).

- `WLS_WSM2`: This is the Managed Server that hosts the Web Service Manager. It listens on the physical IP (`IP2`).

- `WLS_BAM1`: This is the Managed Server that hosts both the BAM Server and the BAM web applications. `WLS_BAM1` is assigned to the logical machine `BAMHOST1`, which runs on the `bamhost1.mycompany.com` host, and its listen address should be `bamvhn.mycompany.com` that resolves to `VIP2`.

- `WLS_BAM2`: This is the Managed Server that only hosts the BAM web applications. `WLS_BAM2` is assigned to the logical machine `BAMHOST2`, which runs on the `bamhost2.mycompany.com` host, and its listen address should be set to `bamhost2.mycompany.com` that resolves to `IP2`.

> Oracle BAM uses a virtual hostname or **Virtual IP** (**VIP**) as the listen address for the Managed Server that hosts BAM Server components (for example, ADC, Report Cache, EMS, and so on). This virtual hostname and corresponding VIP are used for the server migration purpose, in case of server failure. For example, in the event of the `bamhost1` server failure, the virtual IP (VIP2) enabled on `bamhost1` can be switched on a different host (for example, `bamhost2`). After that, you can start `WLS_BAM1` on `bamhost2`. Since the BAM Server still listens on `VIP2`, the failover is transparent from the client's perspective.

The following table is an example of the hostname and IP mapping, which will be used throughout this chapter to demonstrate the BAM HA configuration:

Hostname	IP	Virtual IP	Description
`adminvhn.mycompany.com`		VIP1	`adminvhn.mycompany.com` is the virtual hostname used as the listen address for the Administration Server. This hostname should resolve to `VIP1`, which is the VIP or floating IP address.
`bamvhn.mycompany.com`		VIP2	`bamvhn.mycompany.com` is the virtual hostname used as the listen address for the Managed Server that hosts BAM Server components. This hostname should resolve to `VIP2`, which is the VIP or floating IP address.

Hostname	IP	Virtual IP	Description
`bamhost1.mycompany.com`	`IP1`		`bamhost1.mycompany.com` is the physical hostname of the first node in the cluster. This hostname should resolve to `IP1`, which is the physical IP address.
`bamhost2.mycompany.com`	`IP2`		`bamhost2.mycompany.com` is the physical hostname of the second node in the cluster. This hostname should resolve to `IP2`, which is the physical IP address.

Enabling IPs and VIPs

In a single-node environment, the physical IP of the machine that hosts the BAM Server is used as the listen address. However, in an HA environment, VIPs are required to achieve the IP level virtualization, which is the key in the server migration process.

Enabling IPs and VIPs is platform-specific. In this section, you will learn how to enable IPs and VIPs on Linux.

Perform the following steps to enable IPs/VIPs on Linux:

1. Edit the `ifcfg-<interface:index>` file in the `/etc/sysconfig/network-scripts` directory. `<interface:index>` is the variable that represents the network interface name and its index. For example, edit the `ifcfg-eth0:0` for the first virtual IP, and `ifcfg-eth0:1` for the second VIP on the same **Network Interface Card** (**NIC**).

2. Add the following name value pairs to the configuration file. Modify the values to meet your requirements:

   ```
   DEVICE=eth0:0
   IPADDR=10.0.0.2
   GATEWAY=10.0.0.1
   NETMASK=255.255.255.0
   ```

3. Log in as the root user, and run the following command to start the interface:

   ```
   /sbin/ifconfig <interface:index> up
   ```

To learn more about IPs and VIPs, refer to the corresponding operating system administration guide. There are plenty of resources available on the web as well. For example, the following URL contains tutorials for Linux networking:

```
http://www.yolinux.com/TUTORIALS/LinuxTutorialNetworking.html
```

Configuring shared storage and domain structures

Installing Fusion Middleware on a shared storage allows the same installation to be reused to create domains and the servers in different nodes. In this section, you will learn how to create a shared storage, and how to use the storage location to build domain structures.

Understanding Fusion Middleware home directory structure

The following diagram depicts the Fusion Middleware home directory structure:

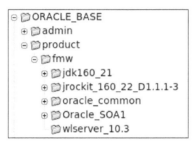

The following table depicts the description of these directories:

Directory	Description
ORACLE_BASE	This environment variable represents the base directory under which the Oracle products are installed (for example, /u01/app/oracle).
Product/fmw	This is the Fusion Middleware home directory, which is represented by the MW_HOME environment variable. It is highly recommended to install MW_HOME on a shared storage, which can be mounted to the ORACLE_BASE/product/fmw directory.
jdk160_21	This is the SUN JDK home directory, which is represented by the JAVA_HOME environment variable.

Directory	Description
`jrockit_160_22_D1.1.1-3`	This is the JRockit JDK home directory.
`oracle_commom`	This directory contains the binaries and library files required by Oracle Enterprise Manager Fusion Middleware Control and **Java Required Files** (**JRF**). The `ORACLE_COMMON_HOME` environment variable is used to represent this directory.
`Oracle_SOA1`	This is the location where the Oracle SOA Suite is installed. The `ORACLE_HOME` environment variable is used to represent this directory.
`Wlserver_10.3`	This is the location where the WebLogic Server binaries are installed. `WL_HOME` is used to represent this directory.

Managing the WebLogic Server domain directories

It is recommended to separate the domain directory for the Administration Server from the domain directory of the Managed Servers. This topology allows a symmetric configuration for Managed Servers, so that you can easily duplicate the domain configurations for Managed Servers across the nodes.

The domain directory for the Administration Server must reside in a shared storage to allow failover to another node with the same configuration. The domain directories for Managed Servers typically reside on a local disk.

The following diagram depicts the recommended domain directory structure in an HA environment:

See the following table for the description of the directory names:

Directory	Description
ORACLE_BASE/ admin/<domain_ name>	This is the root directory for a WebLogic Server domain. When creating this directory, replace the <domain_name> with the actual domain name.
aserver	This directory contains the domain information and the applications for the Administration Server. It includes two sub-directories. One is the Applications directory that contains application ear files, and the other is the domain home directory for the Administration Server, which is represented by the <domain_name> variable.
	This directory and its sub-directories must be created on a shared storage, which allows the Administration Server to fail over to another node in the cluster. The recommended mount point is ORACLE_BASE/admin/<domain_name>/aserver.
mserver	This directory contains the domain information and the applications for the Managed Servers. The Applications directory is the sub-directory that contains application ear files. The <domain_name> sub-directory is the home directory for the Managed Servers.
	This directory and its sub-directories are typically created on a local storage.
<soa_cluster_ name>	This variable represents a directory that is specific to the SOA/ BAM cluster configuration. This directory and sub-directories must be created on a shared storage and mounted to the local disk on ORACLE_BASE/admin/<domain_name>/<soa_ cluster_name>.
dd	This directory contains deployment plans for the WebLogic Server applications. The deployment plans need to be on a shared storage to ensure the proper access by multiple nodes.
fadapter	This directory contains control files that need to be accessed by the file/FTP adapter on multiple nodes.
jms	This directory on a shared storage contains JMS file stores, which ensure the JMS recovery in the case of a server failure or migration.
tlogs	This is the location where JTA transaction logs are stored. This directory is placed on a shared storage for recovery purposes, in the case of a server failure or migration.

> The dd and fadapter directories are specific to the Oracle SOA Suite. You do not need to create such directories if your domain only contains BAM components.

Configuring a shared storage

To meet the HA directory structure requirements, you need to configure a shared storage, which could be either a **Network Attached Storage** (**NAS**) or **Storage Area Network** (SAN) device, and then mount it to the host system using **Network File System** (**NFS**) protocol.

NFS is a platform-independent technology created by Sun Microsystems that allows shared access to the files stored on computers through an interface called the **Virtual File System** (**VFS**) that runs on top of TCP/IP. Computers that share files are considered **NFS servers**, while those that access shared files are considered **NFS clients**. An individual computer can be an NFS server, an NFS client, or both.

Even though it is highly recommended to use an NAS or SAN device as the shared storage solution in the production environment, you can create shared directories on a Linux server for testing purposes. In this section, we will demonstrate how to create the shared storage on Linux for a two-node cluster (bamhost1 and bamhost2).

Creating the oracle user

Perform the following steps to create the oracle user:

1. On both bamhost1 and bamhost2, run the following commands to create the oracle user and the oinstall group, if they do not exist. Note that you must log in as root or a user with admin rights to run these commands:

    ```
    groupadd oinstall
    useradd -g oinstall oracle
    ```

2. On both bamhost1 and bamhost2, execute the id command to verify that the uid and gid attribute of the oracle user are identical on both nodes. Otherwise, use usermod to modify uid/gid.

    ```
    bamhost1> id oracle
    bamhost1> uid=1101(oracle) gid=1000(oinstall)
    groups=1000(oinstall)
    bamhost2> id oracle
    bamhost2> uid=1101(oracle) gid=1000(oinstall)
    groups=1000(oinstall)
    ```

Creating NFS shares

To create shared directories on Linux, perform the following steps:

1. Log in to one of the compute nodes (for example, `bamhost1`) as `oracle`, and create the following directories:

   SHARED_DISK_BASE/product/fmw1

   SHARED_DISK_BASE/product/fmw2

   SHARED_DISK_BASE/admin/<domain_name>/aserver

   SHARED_DISK_BASE/admin/<domain_name>/aserver/applications

   SHARED_DISK_BASE/admin/<domain_name>/<soa_cluster_name>

   SHARED_DISK_BASE/admin/<domain_name>/<soa_cluster_name>/dd

   SHARED_DISK_BASE/admin/<domain_name>/<soa_cluster_name>/jms

   SHARED_DISK_BASE/admin/<domain_name>/<soa_cluster_name>/fadapter

   SHARED_DISK_BASE/admin/<domain_name>/<soa_cluster_name>/tlogs

   Note that SHARED_DISK_BASE is the root for all shared directories. The example code snippets use /u03 to replace SHARED_DISK_BASE.

2. Edit the `/etc/exports` file as the super user (`root`), to export the following directories that you want to remotely access from multiple nodes in the cluster:

   ° SHARED_DISK_BASE/product/fmw1

   ° SHARED_DISK_BASE/product/fmw2

   ° SHARED_DISK_BASE/admin/<domain_name>/aserver

   ° SHARED_DISK_BASE/admin/<domain_name>/<soa_cluster_name>

   A sample configuration looks as follows:

   ```
   /u03/product/fmw1                 *(rw,sync,no_wdelay,insecure_locks,no_root_squash)
   /u03/product/fmw2                 *(rw,sync,no_wdelay,insecure_locks,no_root_squash)
   /u03/admin/soa_domain/aserver     *(rw,sync,no_wdelay,insecure_locks,no_root_squash)
   /u03/admin/soa_domain/soa_cluster *(rw,sync,no_wdelay,insecure_locks,no_root_squash)
   ```

3. Log in as the root user, and run the following command on `bamhost1` and `bamhost2` to export these directories through NFS.

   chkconfig nfs on

   service nfs restart

Mounting shared directories

After these shared directories have been successfully exported, you need to mount them to the machine where BAM is to be installed. On `bamhost1`, mount the shared directories on a remote system to the following mount point:

Mount point	Directories on a remote system (shared storage)
ORACLE_BASE/product/fmw	SHARED_DISK_BASE/product/fmw1
ORACLE_BASE/admin/<domain_name>/aserver	SHARED_DISK_BASE/admin/<domain_name>/aserver
ORACLE_BASE/admin/<domain_name>/<soa_cluster_name>	SHARED_DISK_BASE/admin/<domain_name>/<soa_cluster_name>

On `bamhost2`, mount the shared directories on a remote system to the following mount points:

Mount point	Directories on a remote system (shared storage)
ORACLE_BASE/product/fmw	SHARED_DISK_BASE/product/fmw2
ORACLE_BASE/admin/<domain_name>/aserver	SHARED_DISK_BASE/admin/<domain_name>/aserver
ORACLE_BASE/admin/<domain_name>/<soa_cluster_name>	SHARED_DISK_BASE/admin/<domain_name>/<soa_cluster_name>

To mount these shared directories, perform the following steps:

1. On both `bamhost1` and `bamhost2`, create the following directories as the mount points:

   ORACLE_BASE/product/fmw

   ORACLE_BASE/admin/<domain_name>/aserver

   ORACLE_BASE/admin/<domain_name>/<soa_cluster_name>

2. Edit `/etc/fstab` as the root user.

3. Add the following shared locations and mount points to the `/etc/fstab` file. On `bamhost1`, mount `SHARED_DISK_BASE/product/fmw1`. On `bamhost2`, mount `SHARED_DISK_BASE/product/fmw2`. A sample `fstab` file looks as follows:

```
bamhost1:/u03/product/fmw1               /u01/app/oracle/product/fmw           nfs
rw,bg,hard,nointr,tcp,vers=3,timeo=300,rsize=32768,wsize=32768,actimeo=0 0 0

bamhost1:/u03/admin/soa_domain/aserver       /u01/app/oracle/admin/soa_domain/aserver   nfs
rw,bg,hard,nointr,tcp,vers=3,timeo=300,rsize=32768,wsize=32768,actimeo=0 0 0

bamhost1:/u03/admin/soa_domain/soa_cluster   /u01/app/oracle/admin/soa_domain/soa_cluster   nfs
rw,bg,hard,nointr,tcp,vers=3,timeo=300,rsize=32768,wsize=32768,actimeo=0 0 0
```

4. Log in as the `root` user, and run the following command to mount NFS shares.

```
mount ORACLE_BASE/product/fmw
mount ORACLE_BASE/admin/<domain_name>/aserver
mount ORACLE_BASE/admin/<domain_name>/<soa_cluster_name>
```

Verifying NFS mounts

Run the `touch` command to create a file under the following directories, and verify if these files can be viewed on `bamhost1` and `bamhost2`:

```
touch ORACLE_BASE/product/fmw/test.txt
touch ORACLE_BASE/admin/<domain_name>/aserver/test.txt
touch ORACLE_BASE/admin/<domain_name>/<soa_cluster_name>/test.txt
```

Configuring a WebLogic Server domain for BAM HA

Before you start configuring a WebLogic Server domain for BAM HA, you need to first install Oracle Fusion Middleware Home that hosts the Oracle WebLogic Server and Oracle SOA Suite. To achieve maximum availability, it is highly recommended to use the redundant binary installations on a shared storage. For example, the first Fusion Middleware Home is installed in `SHARED_DISK_BASE/product/fmw1`, and the other redundant home is in `SHARED_DISK_BASE/product/fmw2`.

Install the following Oracle Fusion Middleware components on `bamhost1` and `bamhost2`:

- Oracle Weblogic Server 10.3.4
- Oracle SOA Suite 11.1.1.4.0

After installation, it is recommended to stop all the servers, and then back up the entire Fusion Middleware home directory as follows:

```
bamhost1> tar -cvf fmwbackup.tar MW_HOME
```

Configuring a WebLogic Server base domain

Run the **Configuration Wizard** from the SOA home directory to create a base domain that contains the Administration Server and the Managed Servers for the Web Services Manager.

The base domain architecture is shown in the following diagram:

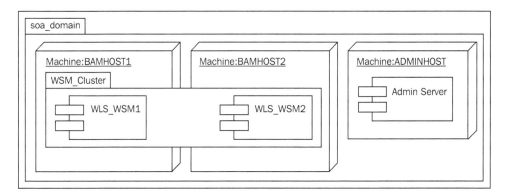

In this diagram, **WSM_Cluster** is the cluster that contains **WLS_WSM1** and **WLS_WSM2**, which are the Managed Servers for Oracle Web Service Manager. **Machine: BAMHOST1, Machine: BAMHOST2**, and **Machine: ADMINHOST** are the logical machines defined in the WebLogic domain-level.

Creating a WebLogic Server domain

First of all, you need to run the **Configuration Wizard** on `bamhost1` to create a base domain. To create a WebLogic Server domain, perform the following steps:

1. Ensure that the BAM repository database is running. For Oracle RAC databases, it is recommended that all instances are running.

2. Execute the following command to start the Oracle Fusion Middleware **Configuration Wizard**:

   `ORACLE_COMMON_HOME/common/bin/config.sh`

3. In the **Welcome** screen, select **Create a new WebLogic domain**, and click on **Next**.

4. In the **Select Domain Source** screen, select **Generate a domain configured automatically to support the following products**, and then select the following components:

    ° **Basic WebLogic Server Domain - 10.3.4[wlserver_10.3]**

    ° **Oracle Enterprise Manager - 11.1.1.0 [oracle_common]**

    ° **Oracle WSM Policy Manager 11.1.1.0 [oracle_common]**

    ° **Oracle JRF - 11.1.1.0 [oracle_common]**

5. Click on **Next**.

6. In the **Specify Domain Name and Location** screen, enter the following:

    ° **Domain name**: Specify the domain name (for example, `soa_domain`).

    ° **Domain location**: Specify the domain location for the Administration Server. For example, enter `ORACLE_BASE/admin/<domain_name>/aserver/`. This directory should be on a shared storage.

    ° **Application location**: Specify the location for applications deployed on the Administration Server. For example, enter `ORACLE_BASE/admin/<domain_name>/aserver/applications`.

7. Click on **Next**.

8. In the **Configure Administrator Username and Password** screen, enter the password for the WebLogic user. Click on **Next**.

9. In the **Configure Server Start Mode and JDK** screen, do the following.

10. **WebLogic Domain Startup Mode**: Select **Development Mode** or **Production Mode**. It is recommended to select **Development Mode** for a development environment and **Production Mode** for a pre-production or production environment.

11. **JDK Selection**: Select **Sun SDK** or **JRockit SDK**. **JRockit SDK** provides better run-time performance and management on production. However, it is highly recommended to test the application with **JRockit SDK** earlier in the project cycle.

12. Click on **Next**.

13. In the **Configure JDBC Components Schema** screen, specify the JDBC connection details for **OWSM MDS Schema**, and then click on Next.

14. In the **Test JDBC Data Sources** screen, ensure that all the connections are tested successfully, and then click on **Next**.

15. In the **Select Advanced Configuration** screen, select the following:
    - ° **Administration Server**
    - ° **Managed Servers, Clusters, and Machines**
    - ° Deployment and Services

16. Click on **Next**.

17. In the **Configure the Administration Server** screen, do the following.
    - ° **Name**: Specify the name of the Administration Server. Keep the default value (**AdminServer**).
    - ° **Listen Address**: Specify `adminvhn.mycompany.com` that resolves to `VIP1`.
    - ° **Listen Port**: Specify the listen port. The default is `7001`.
    - ° **SSL listen port**: Do not specify the listen port for SSL.
    - ° **SSL enabled**: Leave this check box unchecked.

18. Click on **Next**.

19. In the **Configure Managed Servers** screen, click on **Add** to add the following Managed Servers:

Name	Listen address	Listen port	SSL listen port	SSL enabled
WLS_WSM1	bamhost1.mycompany.com	7010	N/A	No
WLS_WSM2	bamhost2.mycompany.com	7010	N/A	No

Note that the physical hostname (`bamhost1.mycompany.com` or `bamhost2.mycompany.com`) is specified in the **Listen address** field.

20. In the **Configure Clusters** screen, click on **Add** to add the following cluster information:

Name	Cluster messaging mode	Multicast address	Multicast port	Cluster address
WSM_Cluster	multicast	239.192.0.0	7001	

Note that `multicast` is the recommended cluster messaging mode when configuring a cluster as multicase is more efficient and more mature than unicast. A multicast address is between `224.0.0.0` and `239.255.255.255`. You can keep the default address (`239.192.0.0`) and its default port (`7001`).

21. In the **Assign Servers to Clusters** screen, assign WLS_WSM1 and WLS_WSM2 to WSM_Cluster.

22. In the **Configure Machines** screen, click on the **Unix Machine** tab and then specify **Node manager listen address** and **Node manager listen port** for each machine that you defined earlier. For example:

Name	Node manager listen address	Node manager listen port
BAMHOST1	bamhost1.mycompany.com	5556 (This is the default value)
BAMHOST2	Bamhost2.mycompany.com	5556
ADMINHOST	localhost	5556

23. Leave all other fields to their default values. Click on **Next**.

24. In the **Assign Servers to Machines** screen, assign servers to machines as follows:

25. In the **Target Deployments to Clusters or Servers** screen, ensure that the wsm-pm application and the oracle.wsm.seedpolicies library are targeted to the WSM_Cluster only. Make sure that all other deployments are targeted to the AdminServer. Click on **Next**.

26. In the **Target Services to Clusters or Servers** screen, ensure that the services in the following table are targeted correctly:

Service	Target
JDBC System Resource (folder)	AdminServer, WSM_Cluster
JOC-Shutdown	WSM_Cluster
JOC-Startup	WSM_Cluster
All remaining services	AdminServer

27. In the **Configuration Summary** screen, click on **Create**.

28. In the **Create Domain** screen, click on **Done**.

Starting the Administration Server

Start the Administration Server using the `startWebLogic` script in the domain directory.

```
bamhost1> ORACLE_BASE/admin/<domain_name>/aserver/<domain_name>/bin/
startWebLogic.sh
```

In `development` mode, the Administration Server automatically creates the `boot.properties` file that enables the server to start without prompting you for the username and password. However, in `production` mode, this file is not present, and you need to manually create this file if you want to use this feature.

Perform the following steps to create the `boot.properties` file:

1. Run the following commands to create the security directory:

    ```
    bamhost1> cd ORACLE_BASE/admin/<domain_name>/aserver/<domain_
    name>/servers/AdminServer
    ```

    ```
    bamhost1> mkdir security
    ```

    ```
    bamhost1> cd security
    ```

2. Create the `boot.properties` file in the `security` directory with the following content:

    ```
    username=weblogic
    password=<password>
    ```

> You can use Node Manager to start and stop the Administration Server. However, it is best practice to start/stop the Administration Server using the `startWebLogic.cmd` on Windows or `startWebLogic.sh` script on Unix/Linux.

Propagating domain directories

As shown in the following table, the domain location for the Administration Server and the Managed Servers are different in a HA environment:

Server name	Domain directory location
The Administration Server	ORACLE_BASE/admin/<domain_name>/aserver/<domain_name>
The Managed Servers	ORACLE_BASE/admin/<domain_name>/mserver/<domain_name>

To separate the domain directory used by the Administration Server from the domain directory used by the Managed Servers on the same host (`bamhost1`), perform the following steps:

1. Run the `pack` command on `bamhost1` to create a template pack as follows:

```
bamhost1> cd ORACLE_COMMON_HOME/common/bin

bamhost1> ./pack.sh -managed=true -domain=ORACLE_
BASE/admin/<domain_name>/aserver/<domain_name>
-template=domaintemplate.jar -template_name=domain_template
```

2. Run the `unpack` command on `bamhost1` to unpack the template in the Managed Server domain directory as follows:

```
bamhost1> cd ORACLE_COMMON_HOME/common/bin

bamhost1> ./unpack.sh -domain=ORACLE_BASE/admin/<domain_name>/
mserver/<domain_name> -template=domaintemplate.jar -app_
dir=ORACLE_BASE/admin/<domain_name>/mserver/applications
```

Perform the following steps to propagate the domain configuration to `bamhost2`:

1. Run the following command on `bamhost1` to copy the template file created previously:

```
bamhost1> cd ORACLE_COMMON_HOME/common/bin

bamhost1> scp domaintemplate.jar oracle@bamhost2:/ORACLE_COMMON_
HOME/common/bin
```

2. Run the `unpack` command on `bamhost2` to unpack the propagated template:

```
bamhost2> cd ORACLE_COMMON_HOME/common/bin

bamhost2> ./unpack.sh -domain=ORACLE_BASE/admin/<domain_name>/
mserver/<domain_name> -template=domaintemplate.jar -app_
dir=ORACLE_BASE/admin/<domain_name>/mserver/applications
```

The `ORACLE_BASE`/admin/<domain_name>/mserver directory must exist before running unpack, and the domain directory structures on `bamhost1` and `bamhost2` must be identical for the pack/unpack commands to work.

Disabling hostname verification for the Administration Server and the Managed Servers

This step is required if you have not set up the appropriate certificates to authenticate the different nodes with the Administration Server. If you have not configured the server certificates, then you will receive errors when managing the different WebLogic Servers using Node Manager, which starts in the secure mode by default.

Perform the following steps to disable host name verification:

1. Log in to the WebLogic Server Administration console.
2. In the **Domain Structure** pane, expand the **Environment** node, and then click on **Servers**.
3. Click on AdminServer(admin) in the **Server** table. The **Settings for AdminServer** page appears.
4. Click on the **SSL** tab and the **Advanced** link.
5. Set **Hostname Verification** to **None**.
6. Click on **Save**.
7. Repeat *steps 3* to *6* for the WLS_WSM1 and the WLS_WSM2 server.
8. Save and activate the changes. You have to restart the Administration Server and all Managed Servers to make the change take effect.

Starting the Node Manager

Perform the following steps to start the Node Manager on bamhost1:

1. Run the ORACLE_COMMON_HOME/common/bin/setNMProps.sh script, which sets the StartScriptEnabled property to true.

    ```
    bamhost1> cd ORACLE_COMMON_HOME/common/bin
    bamhost1> ./setNMProps.sh
    ```

2. Run the following commands to start Node Manager:

    ```
    bamhost1> cd WL_HOME/server/bin
    bamhost1> ./startNodeManager.sh
    ```

Perform the above steps to start Node Manager on bamhost2.

Starting the Managed Servers

Perform the following steps to start the `WLS_WSM1` and `WLS_WSM2` Managed Servers:

1. Log in to the WebLogic Server Administration console.

2. In the **Domain Structure** pane, expand the **Environment** node, and then click on **Servers**.

3. Click on the **Control** tab.

4. Select **WLS_WSM1 and WLS_WSM2**. Click on **Start**.

5. Verify that the **State** column in the **Server** table changes to **RUNNING** for **WLS_WSM1** and **WLS_WSM2**.

Applying the Java Required Files (JRF) template to WSM_Cluster

To apply the JRF template to the WSM cluster, perform the following steps:

1. Log in to Oracle Enterprise Manager Fusion Middleware Control.

2. In the navigation tree, expand **Farm | WebLogic Domain |** `<domain_name>` and select **WSM_Cluster**.

3. Click on **Apply JRF Template** on the right.

4. The confirmation message appears on the screen, which indicates that the JRF template has been successfully applied to the **WSM_Cluster** cluster.

Performing a backup operation

Stop the Administration Server and all Managed Servers, and then perform a backup operation to save your domain configuration in the `ORACLE_BASE/ admin/<domain_name>` directory.

```
bamhost1> tar -cvf base_domain_backup.tar ORACLE_BASE/admin/<domain_name>
```

Extending the base domain to include BAM

In this section, you will extend the base domain to include BAM components. The extended domain architecture is shown in the following diagram:

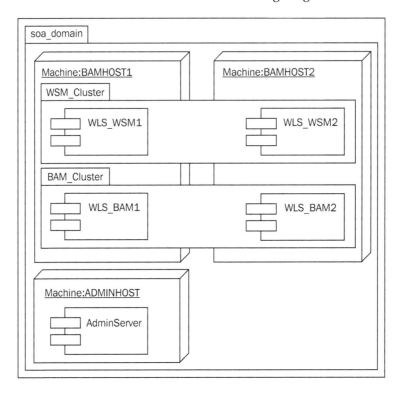

Extending the domain to include BAM

Run the Oracle Fusion Middleware Configuration Wizard on BAMHOST1 to extend the domain as follows:

1. Ensure that the BAM repository database is running. For Oracle RAC databases, it is recommended that all instances are running.

2. Run the `config.sh` command to start the Oracle Fusion Middleware Configuration Wizard.

   `ORACLE_COMMON_HOME/common/bin/config.sh`

3. In the **Welcome** screen, select **Extend an existing WebLogic domain**, and click on **Next**.

4. In the **WebLogic Domain Directory** screen, select the ORACLE_BASE/ admin/<domain_name>/aserver/<domain_name> directory, and click on **Next**.

5. In the **Select Extension Source** screen, select **Extend my domain automatically to support the following added products**, and then select the **Oracle Business Activity Monitoring 11.1.1.0**.

6. Click on **Next**.

7. In the **Configure JDBC Components Schema** screen, specify the JDBC connection details for BAM Schema, and then click on **Next**.

8. In the **Test JDBC Data Sources** screen, ensure that all connections are tested successfully, and then click on **Next**.

9. In the **Optional Configuration** screen, select the following:

   ° **JMS Distributed Destinations**

   ° **Managed Servers, Clusters and Machines**

   ° Deployment and Services

10. Click on **Next**.

11. In the **Select JMS Distributed Destination Type** screen, select **UDD** from the drop-down list for all Fusion Middleware Components' JMS Modules. Note that Oracle does not support using WDD for Fusion Middleware components.

12. In the **Configure Managed Servers** screen, click on **Add** to add the following Managed Servers:

Name	Listen address	Listen port	SSL listen port	SSL enabled
WLS_BAM1	bamvhn.mycompany.com	9001	N/A	No
WLS_BAM2	bamhost2.mycompany.com	9001	N/A	No

Note that the WLS_BAM1 Managed Server's listen address is the virtual hostname (bamvhn.mycompany.com), and WLS_BAM2 listens on the physical hostname (bamhost2.mycompany.com).

13. In the **Configure Clusters** screen, click on **Add** to add the following cluster information:

Name	Cluster messaging mode	Multicast address	Multicast port	Cluster address
BAM_Cluster	multicase	239.192.0.0	7001	

14. In the **Assign Servers to Clusters** screen, assign WLS_BAM1 and WLS_BAM2 to BAM_Cluster.

15. In the **Configure Machines** screen, click on the **Unix Machine** tab, and verify that the following details already exist:

Name	Node manager listen address	Node manager listen port
BAMHOST1	bamhost1.mycompany.com	5556 (This is the default value)
BAMHOST2	bamhost2.mycompany.com	5556
ADMINHOST	localhost	5556

16. In the **Assign Servers to Machines** screen, do the following:

   ° **Assign** WLS_BAM1 to BAMHOST1

   ° **Assign** WLS_BAM2 to BAMHOST2

17. Click on **Next**.

18. In the **Target Deployments to Clusters or Servers** screen, ensure the following deployments targeted correctly:

Deployments	Target
Usermessagingserver and usermessagingdriver-email	BAM_Cluster
usermessaging-xmpp, usermessaging-smpp, and usermessaging-voicexml	Optional
DMS Application	BAM_Cluster, WSM_Cluster, and AdminServer
oracle.rules.* and oracle.sdp.*	BAM_Cluster
wsm-pm and the oracle.wsm.seedpolicies library	WSM_Cluster
oracle.bam*	BAM_Cluster
All remaining deployments	Keep the default target

19. Click on **Next**.

20. In the **Target Services to Clusters or Servers** screen, ensure that the services in the following table are targeted correctly:

Service	Target
mds-owsm*	AdminServer, WSM_Cluster
JOC-Shutdown and JOC-Startup	WSM_Cluster
OraSDPMDatasource* and BAMDataSource	BAM_Cluster
All remaining services	Keep the default target

21. Click on **Next**.

22. In the **Configuration Summary** screen, click on **Extend**.

23. In the **Create Domain** screen, click on **Done**.

24. Restart the Administration Server to enable these changes to take effect.

Performing additional configurations for the BAM domain

In this section, you will perform additional configurations for the BAM domain.

Configuring a JMS persistence store for BAM

In an HA environment, JMS persistence stores should be located on a shared storage. To configure a JMS persistence store, perform the following steps:

1. Log in to the WebLogic Server Administration Console.

2. In the **Domain Structure** pane, expand the **Services** node, and click on the **Persistence Stores** node.

3. In the **Persistence Stores** table, click on the UMSJMSFileStore_auto_<n> persistence store that targets to WLS_BAM1.

4. In the **Configuration** tab, enter the following URL in the **Directory** field:
   ORACLE_BASE/admin/<domain_name>/<cluster_name>/jms

5. Click on **Save and Activate**.

6. Repeat the *steps 3* to *5* for UMSJMSFileStore_auto_<n> that targets to WLS_BAM2.

Configuring a persistence store for transaction recovery

The WebLogic Server uses transaction logs for recovery from system crashes or network failures. To enable the Managed Servers within a WebLogic Server cluster to recover JTA transactions, the `transaction` log must be stored in a shared storage. Preferably, this location should be a dual-ported SCSI disk or on a **Storage Area Network (SAN)**.

To configure a persistence store for transaction recovery, complete the following steps:

1. Log in to the WebLogic Server Administration Console.
2. In the **Domain Structure** pane, navigate to **Environment | Servers**.
3. Click on `WLS_BAM1` in the **Name** column of the table.
4. In the **Configuration** tab, click on the **Services** tab.
5. In the **Default Store** section of the page, enter the following path in the **Directory** field: `ORACLE_BASE/admin/<domain_name>/<soa_cluster_name>/tlogs`
6. Click on **Save**.
7. Repeat *steps 3* to *6* for `WLS_BAM2`.

Untargeting BAM Server components from WLS_BAM2

In the current release, BAM server components, such as ADC, Report Cache, EMS, and so on, do not support active-active deployment in an HA environment. Therefore, you must untarget these components from one of the Managed Servers for BAM. Perform the following steps to untarget the BAM server components from `WLS_BAM2`:

1. In the **Domain Structure** window, navigate to **Environment | Servers**.
2. Click on `WLS_BAM2` in the Name column of the table.
3. Click on the **Deployments** tab.
4. Click on the `oracle-bam` application from the **Name** column of the table.
5. Click on the **Targets** tab.
6. Change the targets for the modules as described in the following table:

Component	Type	Target
oracle-bam (11.1.1)	Enterprise Application	BAM_Cluster
/oracle/bam	WEBAPP	WLS_BAM1
oracle-bam-adc-ejb.jar	EJB	WLS_BAM1
oracle-bam-ems-ejb.jar	EJB	WLS_BAM1

Component	Type	Target
oracle-bam- eventengine-ejb.jar	EJB	WLS_BAM1
oracle-bam- reportcache-ejb.jar	EJB	WLS_BAM1
OracleBAM	WEBAPP	BAM_Cluster
OracleBAMWS	WEBAPP	BAM_Cluster

 You must target all of these components as described in the table. Incorrect targeting can prevent the BAM server from starting.

Propagating domain configurations

After you complete the domain configuration, you need to propagate the domain configuration to `bamhost1` and `bamhost2`, using the `pack/unpack` utility. To propagate the new domain configuration on `bamhost1`, perform the following steps:

1. Run the `pack` command on `bamhost1` to create a template pack as follows:

   ```
   bamhost1> cd ORACLE_COMMON_HOME/common/bin

   bamhost1> ./pack.sh -managed=true -domain=ORACLE_
   BASE/admin/<domain_name>/aserver/<domain_name>
   -template=domaintemplate_BAM.jar -template_name=domain_template_
   BAM
   ```

2. Run the `unpack` command on `bamhost1` to unpack the template in the Managed Server domain directory as follows:

   ```
   bamhost1> cd ORACLE_COMMON_HOME/common/bin

   bamhost1> ./unpack.sh -domain=ORACLE_BASE/admin/<domain_name>/
   mserver/<domain_name> -template=domaintemplate_BAM.jar -app_
   dir=ORACLE_BASE/admin/<domain_name>/mserver/applications
   ```

3. Similarly, to propagate the domain configuration to `bamhost2`, copy the `domaintemplate_BAM.jar` template to `bamhost2`, and run the `unpack` command.

Starting WLS_BAM1 and WLS_BAM2

Perform the following steps to start the WLS_BAM1 and the WLS_BAM2 Managed Servers:

1. Ensure that hostname verification for WLS_BAM1 and WLS_BAM2 is disabled.

2. Ensure that Node Manager is running on bamhost1 and bamhost2. Otherwise, run the WL_HOME/server/bin/startNodeManager.sh command to start the Node Manager.

3. Log in to the WebLogic Server Administration console.

4. In the **Domain Structure** pane, expand the **Environment** node, and click on **Servers**.

5. Click on the **Control** tab.

6. Select WLS_BAM1 and WLS_BAM2. Click on **Start**.

7. Verify that the **State** column in the **Server** table changes to **RUNNING** for WLS_BAM1 and WLS_BAM2.

Applying the JRF template to BAM_Cluster

The monitoring, security, and logging functions in the Enterprise Manager Fusion Middleware Control will not be available unless the JRF template is applied to the cluster.

To apply the JRF template to BAM_Cluster, perform the following steps:

1. Log in to Oracle Enterprise Manager Fusion Middleware Control.

2. In the navigation tree, expand **Farm | WebLogic Domain |** <domain_name> and select **BAM_Cluster**.

3. Click on **Apply JRF Template** on the right.

4. After the confirmation message appears, restart the Administration Server to make the changes take effect.

Performing BAM-specific configurations

In this section, you will perform BAM-specific configuration tasks.

Configuring a cluster address

A **cluster address** is an address that contains a list of the hostnames and ports, which are used by clients to connect to this cluster. BAM web applications and other clients need to use this address to communicate with BAM Server, such as Report Cache and Active Data Cache. Thus, it is a best practice to configure a cluster address for the BAM_Cluster cluster.

As the BAM Server is a singleton, you need to use the server's virtual hostname and port (for example, bamvhn.mycompany.com:9001) as its cluster address.

Perform the following steps to set up a cluster address for BAM_Cluster:

1. Log in to the WebLogic Server Administration console.

2. In the **Domain Structure** pane, expand the **Environment** node, and click on **Clusters**.

3. Click on **BAM_Cluster**.

4. Enter bamvhn.mycompany.com:9001 in the **Cluster Address** field.

5. Click on **Save**.

6. Restart the Managed Server for BAM.

Configuring BAM Web Applications

To configure the BAM Web applications, perform the following steps:

1. Log in to Oracle Enterprise Manager Fusion Middleware Control.

2. In the **Farm_<domain_name>** navigation tree, expand the **BAM** node.

3. Right-click on **OracleBamWeb(WLS_BAM1)**.

4. Select **BAM Web Properties** from the **BAM Web** menu.

5. In the **BAM Web Properties** page, do the following:

6. **Application URL**: This property is used to generate the full URL for reports and alerts. Specify the **Load Balancer** hostname and listen port, for example, http://LBRHostname:port.

7. **Server Name**: Keep the default value (**DEFAULT**).

8. Click on **Apply**.

9. Select OracleBamWeb(WLS_BAM2), and repeat *steps 4* to *6*.

Configuring BAM properties using System MBean Browser

You can use System MBean Browser to configure BAM properties as follows:

1. Select **System MBean Browser** from the **BAM Web** menu.

2. To configure the properties for BAM Web Applications, navigate to **oracle.bam.web | Server | Application | Config | BAMWebConfig**.

3. To configure the properties for BAM Server, navigate to **oracle.bam.server | Server | Application | Config | BAMServerConfig**.

4. To configure the BAM common properties, navigate to **oracle.bam.common | Server | Application | Config | BAMCommonConfig**.

The configuration changes are stored in the corresponding `BAMWebConfig.xml`, `BAMServerConfig.xml`, or `BAMCommonConfig.xml` files, which are located at the `ORACLE_HOME/admin/<domain_name>/mserver/<domain_name>/config/fmwconfig/servers/<server_name>/applications/oracle-bam_11.1.1/config` directory. Note that `<server_name>` refers to the WebLogic Server name for BAM, for example, `WLS_BAM1` or `WLS_BAM2`.

Property settings are server-specific. For example, `BAMWebConfig` settings for `WLS_BAM1` are not propagated to `WLS_BAM2`. Therefore, you need to set up `BAMWebConfig` separately for both `WLS_BAM1` and `WLS_BAM2`.

Backing up your HA environment

Now you can back up your HA environment. To complete this task, stop the Administration Server and all Managed Servers, and perform a `backup` operation to save your domain configuration in the `ORACLE_BASE/admin/<domain_name>` directory.

```
bamhost1> tar -cvf bam_domain_backup.tar ORACLE_BASE/admin/<domain_name>
```

Configuring server migration

Server migration is a process of moving a server instance and its data to another node in case of system failure or server crash. Server migration for Oracle BAM is particularly critical in terms of HA requirements, as BAM Server components in the 11g R1 release, such as Active Data Cache, Report Cache, EMS, and so on, only support running on a single WebLogic Server instance.

In this section, you will learn how to perform server migration for the Administration Server and the Managed Server for BAM.

Configuring migration for the Administration Server

The Administration Server is running on one of the nodes in a cluster. In case of node failure, you need to fail over the Administration Server to another node. This section describes how to fail over the Administration Server from `bamhost1` to `bamhost2`.

The domain directory where the Administration Server is running is on a shared storage, and is mounted from both `bamhost1` and `bamhost2`. The Administration Server is configured to listen on `adminvhn.mycompany.com` that resolves to `VIP1`. To fail over the Administration Server from `bamhost1` to `bamhost2`, you simply need to perform an IP migration, which is to disable `VIP1` on `bamhost1`, and activate it on `bamhost2`. After that, you will be able to start the Administration Server on `bamhost2` with the same VIP.

IP migration is operating system-specific. The following procedure shows how to fail over the Administration Server on Linux:

1. Stop the Administration Server.

2. To disable the VIP address on which the Administration Server listens on `bamhost1`, run the following command as `root`:

   `bamhost1>/sbin/ifconfig <interface:index> down`

   `<interface:index>` refers to the interface, which binds to the VIP address(for example, `eth0:0`).

3. Run the following command on `bamhost2` to activate the same VIP.

   `bamhost2>/sbin/ifconfig <interface:index> <IP_address> netmask <netmask>`

   For example:

   `/sbin/ifconfig eth0:1 10.0.0.1 netmask 255.255.255.0`

4. Test whether you can access the Administration Server on `bamhost2` as follows:

   ○ Ensure that you can access the WebLogic Server Administration console at `http:// adminvhn.mycompany.com:7001/console`.

   ○ Ensure that you can access the Enterprise Manager Fusion Middleware Control at `http://adminvhn.mycompany.com:7001/em`.

To switch the Administration Server back to the original node, perform the same steps to switch the listen IP address (virtual IP or floating IP).

The migration for the Administration Server is a manual process, which requires you to have the `root` privilege. In the next session, you will learn how to use the Node Manager to automatically perform server migration for Oracle BAM.

Configuring server migration for WLS_BAM1

It is highly recommended to configure server migration for WLS_BAM1 on which the singleton BAM Server is running. In the case of WLS_BAM1 server crash or failure, BAM Server services will be brought up automatically on bamhost2, so that BAM Web applications or other clients can continue using the services or interface provided by theBAM Server.

In this section, you will learn how to configure server migration for WLS_BAM1 that hosts both the BAM Server and the BAM Web applications.

Setting up a leasing table for server migration

Perform these steps to create a leasing table for server migration:

1. Create a tablespace called leasing. For example, log on to SQL*Plus as the sysdba user, and run the following command:

   ```
   SQL> create tablespace leasing logging datafile 'DB_HOME/oradata/
   orcl/leasing.dbf' size 32m autoextend on next 32m maxsize 2048m
   extent management local;
   ```

2. Create a user named leasing, and assign it to the leasing tablespace as follows:

   ```
   SQL> create user leasing identified by welcome1;

   SQL> grant create table to leasing;

   SQL> grant create session to leasing;

   SQL> alter user leasing default tablespace leasing;

   SQL> alter user leasing quota unlimited on LEASING;
   ```

3. Copy the WL_HOME/server/db/oracle/920/leasing.ddl file to your database node.

4. Connect to the database as the leasing user, and run the script in SQL*Plus.

   ```
   SQL> @leasing.ddl;
   ```

Creating a data source

Perform the following steps to create a data source that connects to the leasing table:

1. Log in to the WebLogic Server Administration console.

2. In the **Domain Structure** pane, expand the **Services** node, and then click on the **Data Sources** node.

3. Click on **New**, and specify the following properties:

    ○ **Name**: Enter `LeasingDS` as the data source name

    ○ **JNDI Name**: Enter `jdbc/LeasingDS` as the JNDI name

    ○ **Database Type**: Choose the correct database type

4. Click on **Next**, and choose the correct driver.

5. Ensure that the connection pool's initial capacity is set to `0` for this data source.

6. Target the data source to `BAM_Cluster`, and click on **Finish**.

Editing the Node Manager's properties file

The `nodemanager.properties` file is located in the `WL_HOME/common/nodemanager` directory. Edit this file, and add the following properties:

- `Interface`: This property specifies the interface name for the floating IP address. Do not specify the sub-interface, such as `eth0:1` or `eth0:2`. The Node Manager can determine the correct sub-interface name, and bring it up or down automatically.

- `NetMask`: This property specifies the net mask for the interface of the floating IP.

- `UseMACBroadcast`: This property specifies whether or not to use a node's MAC address when sending ARP packets.

A sample configuration in the `nodemanager.properties` file looks as follows:

```
Interface=eth0
NetMask=255.255.255.0
UseMACBroadcast=true
```

Perform this configuration on both `bamhost1` and `bamhost2`. Restart Node Manager, and verify that Node Manager starts successfully.

 As the `nodemanager.properties` file is located on a shared storage, the same interface name (for example, `eth0`) specified in the `nodemanager.properties` file is used by the Node Manager to start Managed Servers on different hosts. However, if a host requires using a different interface or mask, you need to specify these individual parameters in the `JAVA_OPTIONS` environment variable before running the Node Manager script. For example, to use the `eth3` interface on a host, execute the command `export JAVA_OPTIONS=-DInterface=eth3` in a shell, and then start the Node Manager.

Configuring the wlsifconfig.sh script

The WebLogic Server provides a wrapper script (wslifconfig.sh) that can be used to add/remove network alias (virtual IPs) before starting/stopping the Managed Servers. To run the script successfully, you must grant the super user privilege to the Oracle user, and the execute privilege on the /sbin/ifconfig and /sbin/arping binaries.

Perform the following steps to grant these privileges:

1. Log in to bamhost1 as the root user.

2. Add the following configuration to the end of the /etc/sudoers file:

   ```
   oracle ALL=NOPASSWD: /sbin/ifconfig,/sbin/arping
   ```

3. Save the file.

4. Repeat *steps 1* to *3* for bamhost2.

 Do not grant write or execute permission to the /etc/sudoers file. Otherwise, the file cannot be executed successfully.

Configuring server migration targets

Perform the following steps to configure server migration targets in a cluster:

1. Log in to WebLogic Server Administration console.

2. In the **Domain Structure** pane, expand **Environment**, and select **Clusters**.

3. Click on **BAM_Cluster** in the **Name** column of the table.

4. Click on the **Migration** tab.

5. In the **Available** field, select the machines (for example, **BAMHOST1** and **BAMHOST2**) on which migration is allowed.

6. Select the data source (**LeasingDS**) to be used for automatic migration.

7. Click on **Save**.

8. In **Domain Structure** pane, expand **Environment**, and select **Servers**.

9. Select **WLS_BAM1** as the candidate machine for server migration.

10. Click on the **Migration** tab.

11. In the **Migration Configuration** section, select **BAMHOST2** in the **Available** field as the migration target for `WLS_BAM1`.

12. Select **Automatic Server Migration Enabled**.

13. Click on **Save**.

14. Restart the Administration Server and the `WLS_BAM1` server.

Summary

In this chapter, you learned how to configure HA for Oracle BAM in the WebLogic domain level. However, in the real-case scenario, after the completion of setting up the WebLogic Server domain to include BAM HA configuration, you often need to extend your topology to include a load balancer or even an HTTP server.

To learn more about the load balancer and HTTP server configuration for an HA environment, refer to the *Enterprise Deployment Guide*, which is available in the Fusion Middleware documentation library. The URL of this document varies from one release to another. For the 11.1.1.6 release, you can access the *Enterprise Deployment Guide* from the following location:

`http://docs.oracle.com/cd/E23943_01/core.1111/e12036/toc.htm`

In the next chapter, you will learn about the methodologies and some useful techniques for troubleshooting BAM applications.

9
Troubleshooting your BAM Applications

In a typical business flow in BAM, business data moves from various upstream data sources to Oracle BAM, which internally processes and pushes the data to IE browsers for report rendering. As different technologies and BAM Server components are involved, it could be time-consuming and challenging to identify and solve the problem if anything goes wrong in this flow.

As different issues can happen in different product areas and contexts, it is impractical to address all these issues in one chapter. Thus, rather than focusing on the individual issues and the resolutions, the objective of this chapter is to introduce the methodologies for troubleshooting common BAM issues, and provide useful guidelines that can help you to analyze and figure out your own solutions. To illustrate the BAM troubleshooting methodologies and techniques, we will take a look at case studies.

In this chapter, the following topics will be covered:

- Methodologies for troubleshooting Oracle BAM
- Troubleshooting Active Data processing
- Troubleshooting BAM HA issues

Understanding BAM logging and troubleshooting methodologies

In many cases, enabling BAM logging is the prerequisite for troubleshooting BAM issues. It is critical to set up the correct loggers to appropriate levels (for example, SEVERE, WARNING, INFO, CONFIG, FINE, FINER, and FINEST), so that you can collect the information to identify the actual problem, and determine the root cause.

Apart from logging, it is also important to have the proven methodologies in place, so that you can follow these methods/procedures to conduct your troubleshooting practice.

In this section, you will learn the following topics:

- Understanding BAM logging concepts
- Understanding the methodologies for troubleshooting

Understanding BAM logging concepts

BAM provides a set of loggers, which are associated with BAM Java packages/classes. Like Java, these loggers are named by following the dot convention, and are organized hierarchically.

Let's take a look at an example. `oracle.bam.adc` is the root logger for the Active Data Cache. All the loggers for the sub-modules within the Active Data Cache should be named after `oracle.bam.adc`, and therefore become descendants of the root logger. For instance, `oracle.bam.adc.security`, which is the logger that tracks Active Data Cache security logs, is the child logger of `oracle.bam.adc`.

The logging level for the descendant/child (for example, `oracle.bam.adc.security`) inherits from the ancestor/parent (for example, `oracle.bam.adc`) by default, unless its logging level is explicitly specified. Thus, you should be careful when setting a root or parent logger to a low level (for example, `TRACE:32`), which may produce a large amount of log entries in the `log` file.

The following table lists the major root-level loggers for troubleshooting key BAM components:

Logger name	Description
oracle.bam.adapter	This is the logger for troubleshooting the BAM Adapter issues
oracle.bam.adc	This is the logger for troubleshooting the BAM Active Data Cache operations, such as data persistence, ADC APIs, Active Data processing with ADC, and so on
orable.bam.common	This is the logger for debugging BAM common components, for example, BAM Security or BAM Messaging Framework

Logger name	Description
oracle.bam.ems	This is the logger for debugging BAM **Enterprise Message Sources (EMS)**
oracle.bam.eventengine	This is the logger for debugging the Event Engine
oracle.bam.reportcache	This is the logger for debugging the Report Cache
oracle.bam.web	This is the logger for debugging the BAM web applications, which include the Report Server
oracle.bam.webservices	This is the logger for debugging the BAM web services interface

Enabling logging for BAM

To set up loggers for BAM, perform the following steps:

1. Log in to **Enterprise Manager 11g Fusion Middleware Control**.

2. Click on **OracleBamServer(bam_server1)** from the left pane, and select **BAM Server | Logs | Log Configuration**.

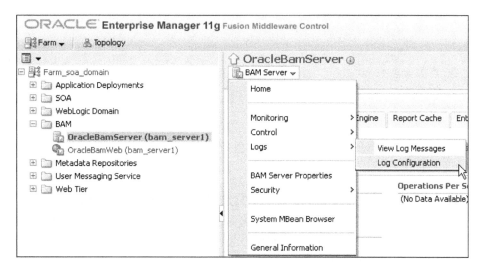

3. Expand **oracle.bam** to set the BAM loggers. To ensure that the log-level changes are persistent, check the checkbox for **Persist log level state across component restarts**.

4. Click on **Apply**.

The logs are written to the `<server_name>-diagnostic.log` file in the `<mserver_domain_dir>/servers/<server_name>/logs` directory. By default, the `log` file follows the size-based rotation policy, and the rotational size is `10M`. You can change the default behavior by editing the `log` file configuration as follows:

1. Log in to **Enterprise Manager 11g Fusion Middleware Control**.

2. Click on **OracleBamServer(bam_server1)** from the left pane, and select **BAM Server | Logs | Log Configuration**.

3. In the **Log Configurations** screen, click on the **Log Files** tab.

4. Select **odl-handler**, and then click on **Edit Configuration**.

5. Edit the `log` file configuration, and click on **OK**.

Setting BAM loggers to appropriate values

Similar to what most Fusion Middleware components do, Oracle BAM uses the log levels specified in the **Oracle Diagnostic Logging** (ODL) standard to control the log details in the diagnostic `log` file.

Similar to the log levels in Java, ODL log levels and their descriptions are listed in the following table:

Log level (Java)	Log level (ODL)	Description
SEVERE+100	INCIDENT_ ERROR:1	This log level enables the BAM Server that reports critical issues or fatal errors.
SEVERE	ERROR:1	This log level enables the BAM Server components to report issues (system errors, exceptions, or malfunctions) that may prevent the system from working properly.
WARNING	WARNING:1	This log level enables the BAM Server components to report events or conditions that should be reviewed and may require actions.
INFO	NOTIFICATION:1	This is the default setting for all the BAM loggers. This log level is used to capture the lifecycle events of BAM Server components and the key messages for notification purposes. For example, if you need to verify the cache location or its running status for the BAM Report Cache, you can set the report cache logger to this log level.
CONFIG	NOTIFICATION:16	This log level enables the BAM Server components to write more detailed configuration information.
FINE	TRACE:1	This log level enables the BAM Server components to write the debug information to the log file. To troubleshoot the BAM server components, you may start with this log level, and increase to FINER or FINEST, if needed.
FINER	TRACE:16	This log level enables the BAM Server components to write a fairly detailed debug information to the log file.
FINEST	TRACE:32	This log level enables the BAM Server components to write a highly detailed debug information.
Inherited from parent		Specify this value if you want a specific logger to inherit the log level from its parent logger.

The default setting for all BAM loggers is `NOTIFICATION:1`. For troubleshooting purposes, it is recommended to set the appropriate loggers to `TRACE:1`, `TRACE:16`, or `TRACE:32`.

> The logging configuration is persisted in the following location on your BAM host: `<domain_dir>/config/fmwconfig/servers/<server_name>/logging.xml`. Theoretically, you can edit this file to modify BAM loggers. However, it is not recommended to do so unless you have a good understanding of the configuration file.
>
> If you have multiple BAM instances in your environment, you can easily duplicate the logging configuration by copying the `logging.xml` file to all BAM instances, rather than making changes through EM.

Introducing the methodologies for troubleshooting BAM

Oracle BAM utilizes different technologies such as EMS, BAM Adapter, Web services, and ODI to integrate different enterprise information systems. Business data received from various data sources are then pushed all the way from the Active Data Cache, through the Report Cache and the Report Server, to Web browsers for rendering reports in real-time. Due to the complexity of the system and various technologies involved, it is critical to use the right troubleshooting methodologies to analyze and resolve issues.

The following are the basic rules of thumb for troubleshooting your BAM applications:

- Understand the BAM key terminologies and architecture
- Identify the problem
- Set up BAM loggers
- Collect the information and debugging

Understanding the key terminologies and the BAM architecture

Understanding the key terminologies and the BAM architecture is a prerequisite for troubleshooting the BAM applications. The key terminologies for BAM include Active Data, Active Data Cache, Report Cache, Report Server, ChangeList, Data Objects, Report, and so on. For more information about these concepts, refer to *Chapter 1, BAM 11gR1 Architecture*.

Identifying the problem

Different issues may require different techniques to troubleshoot. For example, for a report design issue (for example, calculated fields do not show correct values), you should focus on the building blocks for the report design, instead of enabling loggings for the BAM server, which does not provide any help at all.

A BAM issue typically falls into the following categories:

- Report design and report loading (static rendering)
- Report rendering with Active Data (Active Data processing)
- Issues with the key BAM Server components (Active Data Cache, securities, Report Cache, and Event Engine)
- BAM Web applications (Active Viewer, Active Studio, Architect, Administrator, and Report Server)
- Issues with BAM Integration Framework (EMS, Web services APIs, SOA Suite integration, and ODI integration)

To fully identify a problem, you need to first understand the problem description and the category to which the issue belongs. Then, you can gather relevant information, such as the time frame of when the issue happened, the BAM Server release information and patch level, BAM deployment topologies (single node or HA), and so on.

Setting up BAM loggers

Setting up BAM loggers with appropriate logging levels is the key for troubleshooting BAM issues.

BAM loggers can be set up to the following levels (Java logging): SEVERE, WARNING, INFO, CONFIG, FINE, FINER, and FINEST. In a normal situation, all the BAM loggers are set to INFO, by default. In the case of debugging, it is recommended to increase the level to FINER or FINEST.

Loggers contain hierarchies. You need to be careful when setting up root level loggers to FINE, FINER, or FINEST. Suppose that you want to troubleshoot a login issue with the BAM start page using the root logger oracle.bam.adc, which is set to FINEST. In this case, all the descendants that inherit from it have the same logging level. As a result, a large amount of unused log entries are produced, which is not helpful for troubleshooting, and can also impact the overall performance. Therefore, you should set up the corresponding child logger (oracle.bam.adc.security) without enabling the root logger. Collecting information and debugging.

Once the problem is identified and BAM loggers are set up appropriately, it is time to collect the logs to analyze the problem.

The following table lists the files that can be used to troubleshoot BAM issues:

Name	Description
`<server_name>.out`	This is the standard output file redirected by the Node Manager. If the server is started using the `startManagedWebLogic.sh` script directly, you need to refer to the standard output (either the command prompt output or another redirected file specified). This file is located in the following directory: `<mserver_domain_dir>/servers/<server_name>/logs`.
	`<mserver_domain_dir>` refers to the domain home directory for the Managed Server for BAM; `<server_name>` refers to the name of the Managed Server for BAM, for example, `WLS_BAM1`.
	Use this file to collect the server starting information and standard output.
`<server_name>.log`	This log provides information for the WebLogic Server that hosts BAM. This file is located in the following directory:
	`<mserver_domain_dir>/servers/<server_name>/logs`.
`<server_name>-diagnostic.log`	Unlike the `<server_name>.log` file, this log file keeps a track of BAM-specific logs produced by BAM loggers.
	The location of this file is as follows: `<mserver_domain_dir>/servers/<server_name>/logs`.

Debugging actually becomes easier once you have all this relevant information in place. In the next section, you will learn how to use loggers and log files to troubleshoot typical BAM issues.

Troubleshooting the BAM applications

In this section, you will learn how to troubleshoot the BAM Active Data processing issues and the issues around HA.

Troubleshooting the Active Data processing issues

BAM uses the pushed-based mechanism to process Active Data. As illustrated in the following diagram that you saw in *Chapter 1*, the Active Data Cache produces Active Data based on the `ViewSet`, and data changes in associated Data Objects. After that, the Active Data is sent to the Report Cache and then the Report Server for processing:

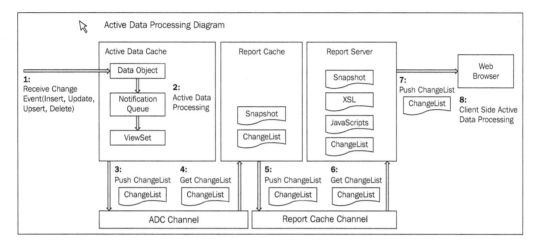

Theoretically, Active Data processing could fail in any step of the flow (Active Data Cache, Report Cache, Report Server, network, or JavaScript issues at the client side). Therefore, in this section of troubleshooting, you will learn the guidelines to test all these components for Active Data issues.

Troubleshooting Report Server issues

At the BAM Server side, Active Data is originally produced in the Active Data Cache, and then pushed forward to the Report Cache and the Report Server. The Report Server is the component that maintains the persistent HTTP connections between the client and BAM Server, and pushes Active Data payloads (`ChangeLists`) asynchronously to the client.

Since Active Data processing in the Report Server is the last step in the processing chain at the server side, the confirmation of a successful Active Data processing in the Report Server implies that Active Data processing in the Report Cache and the Active Data Cache are also successful. Thus, it is best practice to start diagnosing the Report Server first, and then move on to the Report Cache and the Active Data Cache for further analysis.

To diagnose the Active Data issues in the Report Server, enable the loggers as shown in the following table:

Logger name	Description
`oracle.bam.web.reportserver.activedata.ActiveDataPage` (ActiveDataPage)	This logger tracks the push events in the Report Server, and can be used to determine whether the Report Server has successfully pushed the Active Data to the client or not.
`oracle.bam.web.reportserver.activedata.ActiveDataServlet` (ActiveDataServlet)	This logger records asynchronous HTTP request/response-related information, which is useful to debug persistent connections issues between the client and the BAM Server.
`oracle.bam.web.reportserver.activedata.ActiveDataViewSet` (ActiveDataViewSet)	This logger keeps a track of the `ChangeLists` processing details in the Report Server.

Note that the recommended logging level for debugging is `TRACE:32` (`FINEST`).

Enabling ActiveDataPage

To troubleshoot the Active Data processing issues in the Report Server, the first thing to do is set up the appropriate logging level for the `ActiveDataPage` logger. Once this logger is set to `TRACE:32` (`FINEST`), you can then search the `<server_name>-diagnostic.log` file to look for the `flushAllActiveData` or `ChangeList` keywords.

The following is an example of the logs produced by the `ActiveDataPage` logger:

```
ActiveDataPage.flushAllActiveData():
weblogic.servlet.http.RequestResponseKey@2b14d42b, true,
b5bdcb24408df9fbce6c167133c5167bac_7701, 12:31:33 AM,
<script id='s1'>parent.g_oReport.CallProcessActiveData('January 2, 2012 0:31:33',
   'b5bdcb24408df9fbce6c167133c5167bac_7701', 'b5bdcb24408df9fbce6c167133c5167bac-76fe', 1,
'<ChangeList index="1" viewsetID="b5bdcb24408df9fbce6c167133c5167bac-76fe">
   <Group count="3" id="0" level="0" pos="0" xnType="update">
     <Record id="1" pos="0" xnType="update">
       <Field fieldID="2" fieldRefID="0">Greg Masters<FormattedValue>Greg Masters</FormattedValue>
       </Field>
       <Field fieldID="0" fieldRefID="1">Northeast<FormattedValue>Northeast</FormattedValue>
       </Field>
       <Field fieldID="1" fieldRefID="2">200<FormattedValue>200</FormattedValue>
       </Field>
     </Record>
   </Group>
</ChangeList>',
true);RemoveScript();</script>
```

In this example, the `ChangeList` XML payload contains the `index`, the `viewsetID` attributes, and the `Record` of the Data Object (`Employee` Data Object in the `/Samples` folder), which are passed to the client (Web browser) by the Report Server through the invocation of the `ActiveDataPage.flushAllActiveData` method. Thus, you can utilize the `ActiveDataPage` logger and the generated logs to determine whether the Report Server has asynchronously pushed the Active Data to the client successfully.

Enabling ActiveDataViewSet

You should set up the logging level for the `ActiveDataViewSet` logger to `TRACE:32` (`FINEST`), in order to view the `ChangeList` processing information in detail. The log entries typically include the following information:

- `processing index`: This is the index of the `ChangeList` being currently processed

- `last index`: This is the index of the previously processed `ChangeList`

- `strViewSetID`: This is the ID of the `ViewSet` that produces the `ChangeList`

- `strActiveDataSessionID`: This is the ID of the `ActiveDataSession` that is the session context for processing the Active Data

- `strReportID`: This is the ID of the BAM report that is the receipt of the Active Data

- `writing response script to client`: These are the scripts that are passed to the client for processing the Active Data

- `processed index`: This is the index of the `ChangeList` that has been processed

The following is an excerpt of the logs produced by `ActiveDataViewSet`, and you can rely on these logs to collect more information regarding the processing details of the Active Data:

```
inside ActiveDataViewSet.onMessage()...
processing index: 1
last index: 0
strViewSetID = b5bdcb24408df9fbce6c167133c5167bac-76fe
strActiveDataSessionID = b5bdcb24408df9fbce6c167133c5167bac_7701
strReportID = b5bdcb24408df9fbce6c167133c5167bac_7701
writing response script to client: [[
...
]]
processed index: 1
```

Enabling ActiveDataServlet

The corresponding `ActiveDataServlet` java class is the asynchronous Java Servlet that actually pushes the Active Data to the client through the previously established persistent connection when the Active Data arrives in the Report Server.

To debug the `ActiveDataServlet` related issues, set the `ActiveDataServlet` logger to `TRACE:32 (FINEST)`, and then search the `ActiveDataServlet` keywords to look for the information.

The following is an example of the logs produced by the ActiveDataServlet servlet:

```
doRequest: Method = POST; URL = http://bamhost1:9001/OracleBAM/
ActiveDataServlet; Query = null; Session ID = nls4PB8CpvJ3L
KkqvJ1LGG2pp1qMBnTYhTyPtXV3n2xnDF2Qr8n5!1135941767!1325513922380; Is
Session Valid = true; Is Session From Cookie = true; Is Session From
URL = false
```

Right after a new report/dashboard is rendered for the first time, it sends an `HTTP POST` request to the `ActiveDataServlet`, which registers the client (report/dashboard) to ensure it gets called back when the Active Data arrives at the Report Server in the future. Therefore, the previous message typically appears at this time frame, and can be used to troubleshoot the client/server communication issues.

Troubleshooting the Active Data Cache and the Report Cache

The following are the scenarios in which you should consider turning on loggers to troubleshoot Active Data processing in the Active Data Cache or the Report Cache:

- The `ActiveDataPage flushAllActiveData` method is never called to push the Active Data to the client.

- The `ActiveDataPage flushAllActiveData` method is invoked, however, the parameters passed to this method are incorrect. For example, the XML payload for the `ChangeList` is incorrect.

- The error messages in the `log` file indicate that the errors happen in one of the `oracle.bam.adc.*` or `oracle.bam.reportcache.*` modules.

The following table lists the common loggers for the Active Data Cache and the Report Cache:

Logger name	Description
oracle.bam.adc. kernel.viewsets. PushViewset (PushViewset)	This logger tracks the ViewSet and ChangeList related activities, and can be used to verify the push event for ChangeLists.
oracle.bam.adc. kernel.datasets. Dataset (Dataset)	This logger provides you Data Object-related information, for example, the data changes made to the Data Object. You can use this logger to determine if the Data Object operations (Insert, Update, Upsert, and Delete) are successful or not.
oracle.bam. reportcache	This logger keeps a track of the activities in the Report Cache, which can be used to determine the ChangeList and the ViewSet caching issues.

The following are the excerpts of the logs produced by the PushViewset logger:

```
[109] Timer task 1: Pushed changelist 1 for viewset 7fcce3dcef0c2343-
677b43b123bfcc5665-7fd0.
[109] Timer task 1: Completed.
```

As you can see, these logs indicate that changelist 1 for viewset 7fcce3dcef0c2343-677b43b123bfcc5665-7fd0 has been pushed by the Active Data Cache to the Report Cache for further processing.

Troubleshooting the client-side issues

BAM utilizes the asynchronous JavaScript and XML (AJAX) to achieve asynchronous client/server communications and client-side Active Data processing. With AJAX, your BAM report/dashboard can send the initial data to the BAM Server and receive the Active Data asynchronously without having to reload the whole UI.

Using AJAX allows you to build your BAM applications in an effective and efficient way. However, troubleshooting the AJAX aspect of the code is challenging. In this section, you will learn how to debug client-side issues, specifically the JavaScripts for processing the Active Data.

Enabling client-side logging

`ActiveData.js` is the JavaScript that handles Active Data processing at the client side. The following are the scenarios in which you should review client-side logging (logs produced by the `ActiveData.js` JavaScript):

- It is verified that the BAM Server has successfully processed the Active Data, and pushed them to Web browser(s). However, the changes seen on the server side are not reflected in your BAM report/dashboard.

- BAM report views stop refreshing while showing the `Reconnecting...` message in one or more views.

To enable the `AciveData.js` logging, perform the following steps:

1. Open a command prompt on a machine (for example, `bamhost1`) that hosts Oracle BAM. Change the directory to the following:

   ```
   <domain_dir>/servers/<server_name>/tmp/_WL_user/oracle-
   bam_11.1.1.
   ```

   `<domain_dir>` represents the WebLogic Server domain directory for BAM. `<server_name>` refers to the name of the Managed Server for BAM.

2. Locate the `ActiveData.js` file under the current directory. On Unix/Linux, use the `find` command as follows:

   bamhost1> find . -name ActiveData.js

3. The `find` command returns multiple occurrences of `ActiveData.js` as shown in the next screenshot. The highlighted location that contains both the `activedata` directory and a build number (for example, `13846`) is the one you should edit:

```
./eow41x/war/13846/activestudio/scripts/vieweditor/ActiveData.js
./eow41x/war/13846/activestudio/scripts/vieweditor/views/Chart/ActiveData.js
./eow41x/war/13846/reportserver/scripts/activedata/ActiveData.js
./eow41x/war/13846/reportserver/scripts/views/columnar/ActiveData.js
./eow41x/war/13846/reportserver/scripts/views/crosstab/matrix/ActiveData.js
./eow41x/war/13846/reportserver/scripts/views/crosstab/ActiveData.js
./eow41x/war/13846/reportserver/scripts/views/chart/ActiveData.js
./eow41x/war/activestudio/scripts/vieweditor/ActiveData.js
./eow41x/war/activestudio/scripts/vieweditor/views/Chart/ActiveData.js
./eow41x/war/reportserver/scripts/activedata/ActiveData.js
./eow41x/war/reportserver/scripts/views/columnar/ActiveData.js
./eow41x/war/reportserver/scripts/views/crosstab/matrix/ActiveData.js
./eow41x/war/reportserver/scripts/views/crosstab/ActiveData.js
./eow41x/war/reportserver/scripts/views/chart/ActiveData.js
```

4. Make a backup of the following file, and then edit it in a text editor: `/eow41x/war/13846/reportserver/scripts/activedata/ActiveData.js`.

5. Replace all occurrences of the string `// LOG:` with an empty string `""`.

6. Open an **Internet Explorer** (IE) web browser on your client host.

7. In the menu bar, select **Tools | Internet Options**.

8. In the **General** tab, click on the **Delete...** button to clear **Temporary Internet Files** and **Cookies**.

9. Click on the **Security** tab, and then select the **Local** intranet zone.

10. Select the **Custom level...** button.

11. In the **ActiveX controls and plug-ins** section, select **Enable** for every item.

12. Click on the **Internet** zone, and repeat *steps 10 to 11*.

13. Click on **OK** to save all the changes.

With the JavaScript logging enabled, the client-side Active Data processing details are logged in the `ActiveData<timestamp>.txt` file in the `C:\Temp` directory. Search the `ProcessActiveData` or the `ChangeList` keywords in the `log` file, and you should get a result similar to the following:

```
Sep 15 15:17:38 375ms   ###ProcessActiveData:
strViewsetId = 7fcce3dcef0c2343-677b43b123bfcc5665-7fd0; iIndex = 1;
strXml = <ChangeListindex="1" viewsetID="7fcce3dcef0c2343-677b43b123bfcc5665-7fd0">
            <Group id="0" level="0" pos="0">
              <Record id="4" pos="0"xnType="insert">
                <Field fieldID="0" fieldRefID="0"strUnformattedValue="Northeast">Northeast
                  <FormattedValue>Northeast</FormattedValue>
                </Field>
                <Field fieldID="1" fieldRefID="1"strUnformattedValue="John Cooper">John Cooper
                  <FormattedValue>John Cooper</FormattedValue>
                </Field>
                <Field fieldID="2" fieldRefID="2"strUnformattedValue="200">200
                  <FormattedValue>200</FormattedValue>
                </Field>
              </Record>
            </Group>
          </ChangeList>; bIsUpToDate = true
```

This information is similar to what you saw earlier in the server log file. The `ChangeList` XML document is the payload, which is to be processed by the `ActiveData.js` JavaScript. Once it is processed successfully, the client JavaScript should make the changes accordingly in the report view.

Case study

Suppose that you have designed a BAM report/dashboard that contains one or more tab views, and the following issue occurred in one of your environments.

You found that some report views stopped loading or refreshing once the Reconnecting message appeared in one or more views. The initial rendering of the report worked as expected.

Now let's take a look at a case study that showcases how we use the troubleshooting methodologies to diagnose this issue.

Identifying the problem

To accurately and effectively describe the problem, you are required to collect the relevant information from the system. The following is an example of the type of information that you may collect:

- Hardware and software specifications (for example, machine specifications, operating systems, JVMs, Application Server, BAM release information, patching levels, and so on)

- BAM deployment topology (a single node environment or an HA environment)

- The detailed steps to reproduce the problem if applicable

- The BAM Server standard output file (for example, `<server_name>.out`) and diagnostic log file (for example, `<server_name>-diagnostic.log`)

Once you have gathered the required information and identified the problem, you can start diagnosing the issue. The common mistake that most people often make is that they attempt to try different solutions, and hope that they will work without actually understanding the issue and determining possible causes. Our experiences tell us that having a thorough understanding of your environment and the problem itself is the key to diagnosing and troubleshooting problems. For example, you need to first attempt to find out information, such as *when did the issue happen?*, *in what context did the issue occur?*, and so on, before jumping to implement any possible solutions.

Diagnosing the problem

To diagnose a complex issue, you need to figure out a plan that can help you to narrow down the problem, and detect the root cause.

When troubleshooting this particular issue, it is critical to understand why the `Reconnecting...` message is displayed in the report views. To ensure the continuous Active Data processing at the client side, the Web browser must free up its memory consumption and other resources, by executing a function from the `ActiveData.js` JavaScript. As a result, the Web browser will attempt to reconnect the BAM Report Server, and then you will observe the `Reconnecting...` message, which is the indicator of such a reconnecting event. Inside the code of the JavaScript, the `iActiveDataScriptsCleanupFactor` parameter is introduced to specify how frequently this event will be triggered.

After you understand the reconnecting behavior, it is time for us to diagnose the real problem, which is why the Web browser stopped processing the Active Data. As you have learned in the *Troubleshooting the client-side issues* section, you need to enable logging for `ActiveData.js`, and then inspect the log file (for example, `C:\temp\ActiveData<timestamp>.txt`) at the client side.

Search the `MonitorMemoryLeaked` keyword in the `log` file, and you may end up finding the following message:

```
ActiveData: MonitorMemoryLeaked: g_iMemoryLeakThresholdChars =
1048576this.m_iMemoryLeaked = 1049100
```

In this message there are two variables, which are explained as follows:

- `g_iMemoryLeakThresholdChars`: This variable represents a threshold value defined in the `iActiveDataScriptsCleanupFactor` parameter for Oracle BAM. The default value for `iActiveDataScriptsCleanupFactor` is `1048576` (bytes), and you can view and change this parameter in `BAMWebConfig.xml`, which is located in the `<bam_domain_dir>/config/fmwconfig/servers/<server_name>/applications/oracle-bam_11.1.1/config` directory.

- `m_iMemoryLeaked`: This variable represents the total characters (in bytes) of all `ChangeList` payloads that have been processed in `ActiveData.js`.

The `MonitorMemoryLeaked` message is written to the `log` file only when `m_iMemoryLeaked` reaches the threshold value (`1048576` bytes by default) specified in the `iActiveDataScriptsCleanupFactor` parameter. In the meantime, `ActiveData.js` attempts to free up memory consumed by IE, close the previous connection, and then open a new connection to the BAM Report Server.

The default value for `iActiveDataScriptsCleanupFactor` is `1048576` bytes, which is not sufficient in most cases, especially in the production environment. You can set this parameter to a large value (for example, 10 MBs), and you should notice that the `Reconnecting...` scenario does not happen that often after that.

Solution

Tuning `iActiveDataScriptsCleanupFactor` does not completely resolve the issue; however, it does help to narrow down the possible causes, which should be related to the newly established HTTP connection, or the transmission of the messages through the connection. In the end, it is identified that the issue is caused by JavaScript being executed in the same `IFRAME` name, which is shared by two or more tab views. Applying Patch `12419288` on top of the 11.1.1.4 release should fix the problem. If you are on 11.1.1.6 or any later releases, the issue is already fixed, and no patches are needed.

In summary, this case demonstrates how to use the methodology to troubleshoot a complex issue, and the importance of enabling JavaScript logging in the scenario of client-side Active Data processing.

Troubleshooting BAM HA issues

In a BAM HA environment, the common issues you might encounter are as follows: one Managed Server for BAM cannot start up, the BAM start page or report cannot be accessed using the load balancer URL, the BAM Server is down and does not fail over to another node, and so on. These issues are BAM HA configuration-related.

The majority of BAM HA issues that we have seen are configuration-related, and are typically caused by inappropriate configuration in the WebLogic Server domain-level or BAM components-level.

The following are the guidelines to troubleshoot such HA issues:

- Understanding the BAM HA topology
- Inspecting `log` files for the Managed Server for BAM
- Setting up appropriate loggers

Understanding the topology is critical for troubleshooting HA issues. In a typical BAM HA environment, you need to review the WebLogic domain topology, and collect the following key information:

- Collecting BAM cluster information, such as the cluster address, cluster messaging mode (Unicast or Multicast), servers that are assigned to the cluster (for example, WLS_BAM1 and WLS_BAM2), and so on

- Identifying the WLS Server instance (for example, WLS_BAM1 or WLS_BAM2) on which the BAM Server components are running

- Verifying BAM deployment

Inspecting log files is a must for troubleshooting BAM issues in an HA environment. The following table lists the files that can be used to troubleshoot these issues:

Name	Description
<server_name>.out	This file can be found in the following directory: <mserver_domain_dir>/servers/<server_name>/logs.
	<mserver_domain_dir> refers to the domain home directory for the Managed Server for BAM, for example, ORACLE_BASE/admin/<domain_name>/mserver/<domain_name>.
	<server_name> refers to the name of the Managed Server for BAM, for example, WLS_BAM1.
<server_name>-diagnostic.log	The location of this file is as follows: <mserver_domain_dir>/servers/<server_name>/logs.
	Use this log file to troubleshoot issues with BAM server components (for example, securities, ADC, and so on)

There are no specific loggers for debugging HA issues, especially configuration issues. However, some BAM components, such as Active Data Cache or Messaging Framework, may throw exceptions at runtime. To debug such BAM-specific issues, enabling loggers will help to identify the problem.

Case study

In this case study, you will learn how to troubleshoot a typical BAM HA startup issue.

Identifying the problem

In an HA environment that contains both the Managed Server for BAM and the Managed Server for SOA, if the Managed Server for BAM is started before the Managed Server for SOA, an authentication error happens when trying to log in to the BAM start page. The login issue gets resolved by restarting the Managed Server for BAM.

Diagnosing the problem

To analyze this problem, you need to first review the HA topology. In this case, the Weblogic Server domain contains the Manager Servers for both BAM and SOA.

After this, you need to review the `<server_name>-diagnostic.log` file, which shows the following snippets:

```
Caused by: java.security.AccessControlException: access denied
(oracle.security.jps.service.policystore.PolicyStoreAccessPermission
Context:APPLICATION Context Name:soa-infra Actions:getApplicationPolicy)
at java.security.AccessControlContext.checkPermission(AccessControlConte
xt.java:323)
```

The underlined code indicates that the issue is related to the policy store configuration. By default, BAM stores its policies and application roles in the file-based policy store, which is `system-jazn-data.xml` in the `<mserver_domain_dir>/config/fmwconfig` directory. Note that `<mserver_domain_dir>` refers to the domain directory for the Managed Server, and is different than the `<aserver_domain_dir>`, which represents the domain directory for the Administration Server.

When the BAM server is started, it initiates the default policies and application roles in `system-jazn-data.xml` if they do not exist in the policy store. When SOA server gets started, it appends the SOA-related policies and application roles to the same file. However, in an HA environment, these BAM security information may get overwritten by SOA, or vice versa.

What happens in this scenario is that there are two `system-jazn-data.xml` files located in the `<mserver_domain_dir>/config/fmwconfig` directory and the `<aserver_domain_dir>/config/fmwconfig` directory, respectively. When BAM is started from the `<mserver_domain_dir>` location, these BAM security details are only written to the file in the `<mserver_domain_dir>/config/fmwconfig` directory. As the original `system-jazn-data.xml` file resided in `<aserver_domain_dir>`, is not updated, it overwrites the same file in `<mserver_domain_dir>` when the Managed Server for SOA is started.

Solution

Once the root cause is determined, it is time to work out the solution.

The ideal solution is to use a centralized policy store, which can be either OID or Oracle Database-based. To learn more about the policy store configuration, refer to the *Enterprise Deployment Guide*.

If you don't want to use a centralized policy store to store the policies and the application roles, you need to perform the following steps to solve this problem:

1. Use the WebLogic Server script (for example, `startManagedWebLogic.sh`) in the `<aserver_domain_dir>` directory to start the Managed Server for SOA and the Managed Server for BAM separately, which ensures that `<aserver_domain_dir>/config/fmwconfig/system-jazn-data.xml` contains the policies and the application roles for both SOA and BAM.

2. Stop both the Managed Servers.

3. Delete the the `oracle-bam_11.1.1` directory from the following location: `<aserver_domain_dir>/config/fmwconfig/servers/<server_name>/applications`.

4. Start both the Managed Servers from the `<mserver_domain_dir>` directory. This ensures that the `system-jazn-policy.xml` file is copied from the `<aserver_domain_dir>/config/fmwconfig` directory to the `<mserver_domain_dir>/config/fmwconfig` directory.

> Oracle BAM has three configuration files, which are `BAMCommonConfig.xml`, `BAMWebConfig.xml`, and `BAMServerConfig.xml`, located in the `<domain_dir>/config/fmwconfig/servers/<server_name>/applications/oracle-bam_11.1.1/config` directory. As it is recommended to create two separate domain directories for the Administration Server and the Managed Server for BAM, you need to ensure that such configuration files only exist in the `<mserver_domain_dir>` directory.

Summary

It is obvious that troubleshooting the BAM applications varies from one system to another. However, the troubleshooting methodologies and guidelines remain the same. So, in the chapter, we focused more on methodologies and troubleshooting guidelines, so that you can apply the techniques used in the case study to real-world scenarios.

To summarize, in order to troubleshoot BAM applications, you need to understand its architecture and key concepts, and then analyze logs and other related information to find the solution.

10
Building your Reports Using ADF

In previous chapters, you learned the technologies for building a report using the Active Viewer. However, these views can only be rendered in Internet Explorer, as it requires IE-specific XML and Active Data processing. BAM 11g provides a **preview** feature that allows users to create ADF-based views. Once these views are deployed to an Application Server, they can be accessed using any web browsers.

In this chapter, you will learn how to create your report using ADF.

ADF – an overview

Oracle **Application Development Framework** (ADF) is a framework that implements the MVC design pattern. Oracle ADF builds on the latest Java EE standards and various open source technologies, to standardize and simplify enterprise application development.

The high-level ADF architect is as follows:

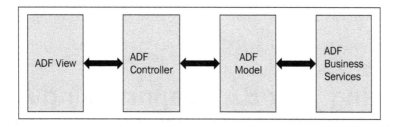

This multi-layer architecture contains the following components:

- **ADF Business Services**: This layer provides business logics and interfaces for interacting with backend information systems. ADF Business Services layer may contain Java classes, Enterprise Java Beans, SOA composites, BAM, web services, ADF Business Components, and so on.

- **ADF Model**: The ADF Model represented by Data Controls in the JDeveloper IDE, provides an abstraction of business interface that internally utilizes data bindings (ADF Bindings) to connect to the various underlying business services. ADF Binding is in compliance with **JSR-227**.

- **ADF Controller**: ADF controller is used to control page flows, which involves UI inputs and interactions.

- **ADF Faces**: ADF Faces are the actual view components that render user interfaces.

The following diagram illustrates the high-level architecture in the scenario of creating a BAM View using ADF. BAM Data Objects are the actual Business Services. BAM Data Control is the ADF Model that uses ADF Bindings to connect to Data Objects. ADF Faces are the view components that implement different view types (tables, graphs, list, forms, and so on).

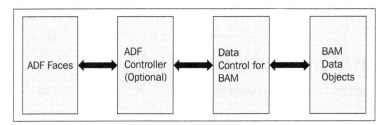

This section only covers an overview of the Oracle ADF. To learn more about ADF and its related technologies, refer to the *Fusion Developer's Guide for Oracle Application Development Framework*, which is available in the *Fusion Middleware* document library. For the 11.1.1.6 release, this document can be accessed at the following URL:

```
http://docs.oracle.com/cd/E23943_01/web.1111/b31974/toc.htm
```

Designing your BAM report using ADF

ADF provides technologies, such as ADF Bindings and JSF pages, which can be used to retrieve and render business data in real time. Unlike views built on Active Viewer, to access ADF based reports, you need to deploy your ADF application to an Application Server first.

In this section, you will learn how to build a simple ADF view (bar chart) to display a BAM Data Object.

Developing your report using ADF

To develop an ADF-based BAM report, you need to complete the following steps:

1. Create an ADF project in JDeveloper.

2. Configure your BAM connections.

3. Create a BAM Data Control.

4. Create a JSF page and data binding.

Creating an ADF project in JDeveloper

Perform the following steps to create a new project in JDeveloper:

1. Open a command prompt and change the directory to `FMW_HOME/jdeveloper/jdev/bin`.

2. Run the following command to start the JDeveloper IDE in the `PREVIEW` mode:

   `./jdev -J-DPREVIEW_MODE=true`

3. In the `JDeveloper` menu, select **File | New...**. The **New Gallery** screen appears.

4. Select **Applications** in the **Categories** pane, and select **Generic Application** in the **Items** pane:

5. Click on **OK**. The **Create Generic Application** window appears.

6. In the first step, specify the application name and location. Click on **Next**.

7. In the **Name your project** screen, do the following:

    ○   Enter the project name (for example, ADFViewsProject). Keep the project directory as default.

    ○   Move **ADF Faces**, **ADF Page Flow**, **HTML**, and **XML** from the **Available:** list to the **Selected:** list. Note that selecting **ADF Faces**, automatically selects **Java**, **JSF**, **JSP** and **Servlets**.

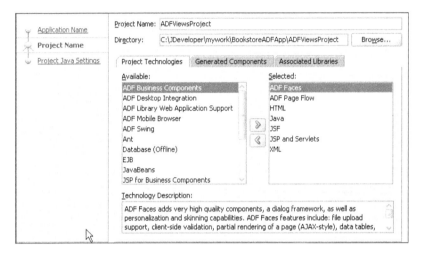

8. Click on **Next**.

9. In the **Configure Java Settings** screen, specify the package name, for example bookstore.adf.

10. Click on **Finish**.

11. Now you should see the ADFViewsProject project and its structures in **Application Navigator** as shown in the following screenshot:

12. Click on **Save All** to save the entire project.

Configuring your BAM connection

In the **Application Resources** pane, ensure that a BAM server connection has been established. Otherwise, perform the following steps to configure a new BAM connection:

1. Ensure that the Administration Server and the Managed Server for BAM are up and running.

2. In the **Application Resources** pane, right-click on **Connections**, then click on **New Connection | BAM....** The BAM **Connection Wizard** appears.

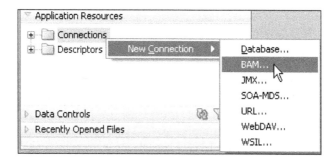

3. In the **Name** screen, select **Application Resources**, and enter a name for the connection. Click on **Next**.

4. In the **Connection** screen, enter the BAM server connection details as follows:

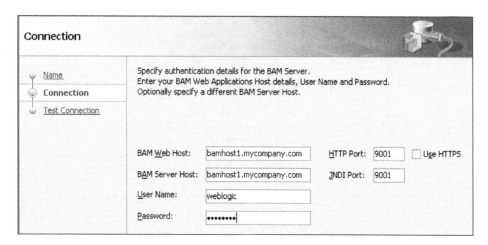

5. Click on **Next**.

6. In the **Test Connection** screen, click on **Test connection**, and verify the test results as shown in the following screenshot:

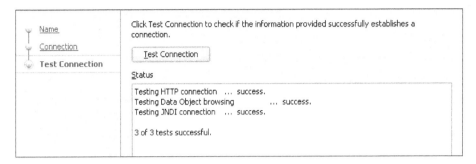

7. Click on **Finish**.

Creating BAM Data Control for a Data Object

The BAM Data Control provides the interfaces for BAM operations. The following steps illustrate how to create a BAM Data Control for the /BookstoreDemo/order Data Object:

1. In the **Application Resources** pane, expand the **BAM** node, and navigate to the **BAM** folder that contains the Data Object:

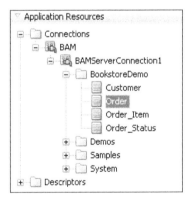

2. Right-click the **Order** Data Object, and select **Create Data Control**. The **Create BAM Data Control** wizard opens:

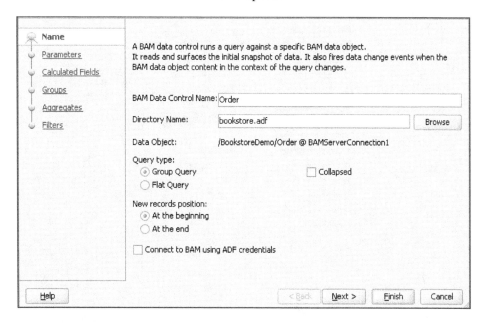

3. Change the Data Control name to `OrderDC`. Select **Group Query** for the **Query type:**, and click on **Next**.

4. Click on **Next** to skip the **Parameters** and **Calculation Fields** page.

5. In the **Groups** page, select a group by field (for example, `OrderStatusCode`), and click on **Next**:

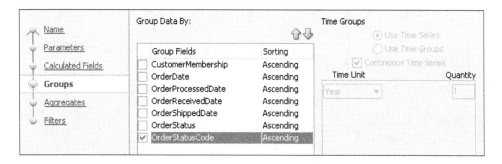

6. In the **Aggregates** page, specify **Aggregates** to count the number of orders as shown in the following screenshot:

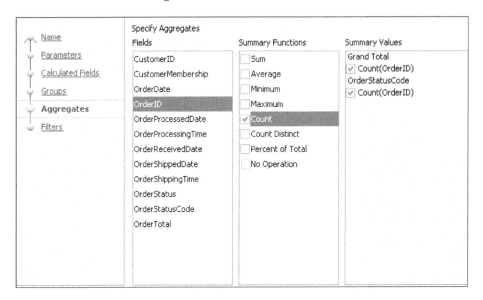

7. Click on **Finish**. In the **Data Controls** pane, you should see the BAM Data Control that shows the name, its queries, and associated parameters. In this example, **_OrderStatusCode** is the group query name; **COUNT_OrderID**, **id**, and **value** are the parameters for the query:

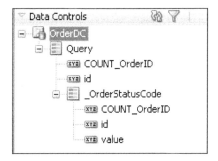

8. Click on **Save All**.

Creating a JSF page and data binding

In this section, you will first create an empty JSF page, and bind the BAM data control to this page. This allows the ADF view to render with Active Data. To achieve this, perform the following steps:

1. In the **JDeveloper** menu, select **File | New...**. The **New Gallery** screen appears.

2. Select **JSF** in the **Categories** pane, and **JSF Page** in the **Items** pane.

3. Click on **OK**. The **Create JSF Page** wizard opens.

4. Enter the file name (for example, `view1.jspx`), and ensure that **Create as XML Document (*.jspx)** is selected.

5. Click on **OK**. The empty JSF page opens in the **Design** view.

6. In the **Data Controls** pane, expand the Data Control you created earlier. Drag-and-drop the _**OrderStatusCode** node to the panel in the **Design** view:

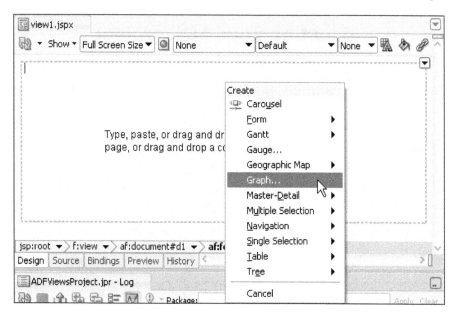

7. In the menu, select **Graph...**. The **Component Gallery** wizard opens.

8. Click the bar chart, and then click on **OK**. The **Create Bar Graph** wizard opens.

9. Select the **Count_OrderID** in the **Bars** field and **value** in the **X Axis** field. Click on **OK**:

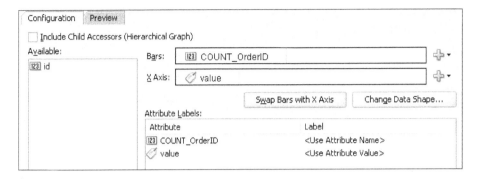

10. You should see the bar charts in the **Design** view.

11. Click on **Save All**.

Deploying and testing your ADF project

Configuring the Application Server runtime environment is the prerequisite for deploying and testing. There are multiple approaches to prepare such an environment. However, using the JDeveloper integrated WebLogic Server is the easiest way to test your ADF project. If you want to deploy your project to a remote Application Server, you have to install the ADF libraries into that environment. Otherwise, the application won't run properly.

As the integrated WebLogic Server running the ADF view needs to connect to the BAM Server in another domain to move data to the ADF views, you have to enable the cross-domain security to allow two different domains to interact with each other.

Perform the following steps to configure the trust domains:

1. In the **JDeveloper** menu, click on **Run | Start Server Instance**.

2. Log in to the WebLogic Server Console at `http://127.0.0.1:7101/console`. The default username/password is `weblogic/weblogic1`.

3. In the **Domain Structure** pane, click on the domain name.

4. In the **Security** tab, select **Cross Domain Security Enabled**.

5. Expand the **Advanced** section. Set up the credential and confirm it. Note that the credential can be anything as long as they are the same on all the servers.

6. Click on **Save**.

7. Repeat steps 2 to 6 to configure the trusted domain for the Managed Server for BAM. You must use the same credentials for all the servers.

To run the `view1.jspx` JSF page that you created earlier in the integrated WebLogic Server, do the following:

1. In the **Application Navigation**, right-click on the `view1.jspx` JSF page, and click on **Run**.

2. The project is deployed to the integrated server. After the deployment finishes, the following URL is opened in a web browser:
   `http://127.0.0.1:7101/BookstoreADFApp-ADFViewsProject-context-root/faces/view1.jspx`

3. You should see the bar chart as shown in the next screenshot. Unlike the BAM reports created in BAM Active Studio, the ADF-based Views can be rendered in any web browsers.

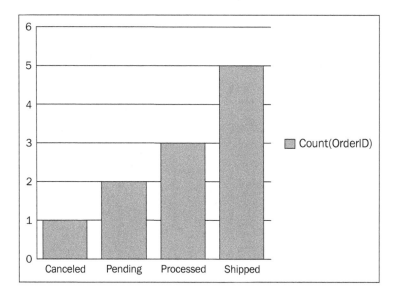

Summary

In this chapter, you learned how to build your BAM report using ADF. As an ADF or Java EE developer, you may see the beauty of this approach. However, you need to be aware that the ADF-based report is a preview feature, which means Active Studio is still the preferred tool for building reports, especially for production.

Index

Symbols

3D bar chart View
  used, for creating BAM report 35-37
.jca file 47
<soa_cluster_name> directory 153
.wsdl file 47
.xsd file 47

A

actions 87
Active Data
  about 11
  processing 15
Active Data Cache (ADC)
  about 14
  services 14
  troubleshooting 192, 193
Active Data Cache (ADC), services
  Active Data, processing 15
  BAM artifacts, maintaining 14
  data models, managing 15
  persistence 14
ActiveDataPage
  enabling 190, 191
ActiveDataPage flushAllActiveData
    method 192
Active Data processing
  testing 102, 103
Active Data processing issues
  Active Data Cache, troubleshooting 192
  client-side issues, troubleshooting 193
  Report Cache, troubleshooting 192
  troubleshooting 189

ActiveDataServlet
  enabling 192
ActiveDataViewSet
  enabling 191
  log entries 191
ActiveStudio permission 120
ActiveViewer permission 120
ADCServerName property 34
ADCServerPort property 34
ADF
  about 203
  architect 203
  components 204
  multi-layer architecture 204
  used, for building BAM report 204
ADF-based BAM report, developing
  ADF project, creating in JDeveloper 205, 206
  ADF project, deploying 212, 213
  ADF project, testing 212, 213
  BAM connection, configuring 207
  BAM Data Control, creating 208-210
  data binding, creating 211
  JSF page, creating 211
ADF Business Services 204
ADF components
  ADF Business Services 204
  ADF Controller 204
  ADF Faces 204
  ADF Model 204
ADF Controller 204
ADF Faces 204
ADF Model 204
ADF project
  creating, JDeveloper 205, 206
  deploying 212, 213
  testing 212, 213

D

data
  sending, to BAM through Oracle BAM
    Adapter 50-52
database commands
  used, for BAM data migration 138, 139
databases, HA environment
  database parameters, setting up 147
  database schemas, installing for
    SOA/BAM 146
  transactional recovery privileges,
    granting 147
data binding
  creating 211
data manipulation tasks, BAM report
    designs
  calculated fields, adding 78
  filter expression, creating 74, 75
  filters, adding 73
  parameters, defining 75, 76
  performing 73
  surface prompts, configuring 77
data mappings and transformations
  testing 95
data migration
  BAM data, migrating using database
    commands 138, 139
  BAM data, migrating using EXPORT
    command 140, 141
  BAM data, migrating using ICommand 140
  BAM data, migrating using IMPORT
    command 143, 144
  performing 138
data models
  managing 15
Data Object
  about 7, 8
  creating, BAM Architect used 27
  date time 7
  designing 22
  extending, with calculated fields 28
  extending, with lookup fields 28
  external Data Objects, using 31
  float 7
  importing, ICommand used 33

integer 7
  lookup fields, adding 30, 31
  mapping, to internal database tables 26
  string 7
Data Object design considerations 24, 25
Data Object, designing
  BAM Architect Web application 22
  design considerations 24, 25
  subfolders, creating 23, 24
Data Object field types
  auto-incrementing integer 26
  boolean 26
  Calculated 26
  DateTime 26
  decimal 26
  float 26
  integer 26
  string 26
  Timestamp 26
DataobjectName property 50
Data Object operation properties
  Batching 59
  configuring 59
  Data Object Name 59
  Operation 59
  Transaction 59
DataObjectOperationsByID
    webservice API 45
DataObjectOperationsByName web service
  about 67
  using 68, 69
Data Objects and fields, BAM
    report designs
  specifying 72
dataset, BAM 25
DatasetField element 9
dd directory 153
DefaultAuthenticator 113
DEPENDENCIES parameter 141
detail View
  creating 81, 82
Distinguished Name (DN) 114
domain architecture, Oracle BAM
  about 148
  AdminServer 148
  WLS_BAM1 149

X

Thank you for buying
Oracle BAM 11gR1 Handbook

About Packt Publishing

Packt, pronounced 'packed', published its first book "Mastering phpMyAdmin for Effective MySQL Management" in April 2004 and subsequently continued to specialize in publishing highly focused books on specific technologies and solutions.

Our books and publications share the experiences of your fellow IT professionals in adapting and customizing today's systems, applications, and frameworks. Our solution based books give you the knowledge and power to customize the software and technologies you're using to get the job done. Packt books are more specific and less general than the IT books you have seen in the past. Our unique business model allows us to bring you more focused information, giving you more of what you need to know, and less of what you don't.

Packt is a modern, yet unique publishing company, which focuses on producing quality, cutting-edge books for communities of developers, administrators, and newbies alike. For more information, please visit our website: www.packtpub.com.

About Packt Enterprise

In 2010, Packt launched two new brands, Packt Enterprise and Packt Open Source, in order to continue its focus on specialization. This book is part of the Packt Enterprise brand, home to books published on enterprise software – software created by major vendors, including (but not limited to) IBM, Microsoft and Oracle, often for use in other corporations. Its titles will offer information relevant to a range of users of this software, including administrators, developers, architects, and end users.

Writing for Packt

We welcome all inquiries from people who are interested in authoring. Book proposals should be sent to author@packtpub.com. If your book idea is still at an early stage and you would like to discuss it first before writing a formal book proposal, contact us; one of our commissioning editors will get in touch with you.

We're not just looking for published authors; if you have strong technical skills but no writing experience, our experienced editors can help you develop a writing career, or simply get some additional reward for your expertise.

Oracle Service Bus 11g Development Cookbook

ISBN: 978-1-84968-444-6   Paperback: 522 pages

Over 80 practical recipes to develop service and message-oriented solutions on the Oracle Service Bus

1. Develop service and message-oriented solutions on the Oracle Service Bus following best practices using this book and ebook

2. Extend your practical knowledge of building solutions on the Oracle Service Bus

3. Packed with hands-on cookbook recipes, with the complete and finished solution as an OSB and SOA Suite project, made available electronically for download

Oracle JDeveloper 11gR2 Cookbook

ISBN: 978-1-84968-476-7   Paperback: 406 pages

Over 85 simple but incredibly effective recipes for using Oracle JDeveloper 11gR2 to build ADF applications

1. Encounter a myriad of ADF tasks to help you enhance the practical application of JDeveloper 11gR2

2. Get to grips with deploying, debugging, testing, profiling and optimizing Fusion Web ADF Applications with JDeveloper 11gR2 in this book and e-book

3. A high level development cookbook with immediately applicable recipes for extending your practical knowledge of building ADF applications

Please check **www.PacktPub.com** for information on our titles

Oracle BI Publisher 11g: A Practical Guide to Enterprise Reporting

ISBN: 978-1-84968-318-0   Paperback: 254 pages

Create and deliver improved snapshots in time of your Enterprise data using Oracle BI Publisher 11g

1. A practical tutorial for improving your Enterprise reporting skills with Oracle BI Publisher 11g

2. Master report migration, template design, and E-Business Suite integration

3. A practical guide brimming with tips about all the new features of the 11g release

Oracle BI Publisher 11g: A Practical Guide to Enterprise Reporting

Create and deliver improved snapshots in time of your Enterprise data using Oracle BI Publisher 11g

Daniela Bozdoc

Oracle Weblogic Server 11gR1 PS2: Administration Essentials

ISBN: 978-1-84968-302-9   Paperback: 304 pages

Install, configure, deploy, and administer Java EE applications with Oracle WebLogic Server

1. A practical book with step-by-step instructions for admins in real-time company environments

2. Create, commit, undo, and monitor a change session using the Administration Console

3. Create basic automated tooling with WLST

4. Access advanced resource attributes in the Administration Console

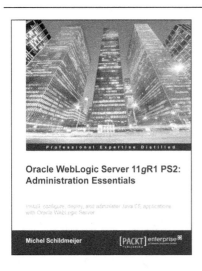

Oracle WebLogic Server 11gR1 PS2: Administration Essentials

Install, configure, deploy, and administer Java EE applications with Oracle WebLogic Server

Michel Schildmeijer

Please check **www.PacktPub.com** for information on our titles

www.ingramcontent.com/pod-product-compliance
Lightning Source LLC
LaVergne TN
LVHW062313060326
832902LV00013B/2184